MASTERS OF FX

MASTERS OF FX

Behind the Scenes with Geniuses of Visual and Special Effects

Ian Failes

Forewords by James Cameron
Director of **Avatar, Titanic, Aliens** and **The Terminator**

and Lorenzo di Bonaventura
Producer of **Constantine, Red** and **Transformers**

ilex

Masters of FX

An Hachette UK Company www.hachette.co.uk

First published in Great Britain in 2015 by
ILEX, a division of Octopus Publishing Group Ltd
Octopus Publishing Group
Carmelite House
50 Victoria Embankment
London, EC4Y 0DZ
www.octopusbooks.co.uk
Design, layout, and text copyright
© Octopus Publishing Group 2015
Images © their respective copyright holders

Publisher: Roly Allen
Senior Project Editor: Natalia Price-Cabrera
Senior Specialist Editor: Frank Gallaugher
Assistant Editor: Rachel Silverlight
Commissioning Editor: Zara Larcombe
Art Director: Julie Weir
Book Design and Layout: Grade Design
Senior Production Manager: Marina Maher

ISBN 978-1-78157-267-2

A CIP catalogue record for this book is available
from the British Library

Printed and bound in China

10 9 8 7 6 5 4 3 2 1

Contents >

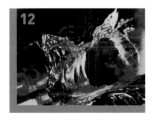

Foreword > by James Cameron

Leading Hollywood director, film producer, screenwriter, editor, and inventor

[1] James Cameron on the set of **Avatar**.

This book celebrates 16 masters of visual effects. I know most of them personally, and seven of them I've worked with over the years. A few I consider close friends. Though they know me as a director, I actually started out in their game, doing visual effects on low-budget movies, so they also know me as someone who talks their language. This makes me both sympathetic and responsive to their needs but also demanding, because I know what's possible. Often the job requires knowing not just what's possible, but what CAN be possible, because we are constantly inventing to bring the impossible to life on the screen.

The masters in this book are collectively responsible for some of the most stunning images ever projected on the world's screens. They have transported audiences to realms of fantasy and brought fantastic creatures and characters to life that are so iconic they are indelible parts of our shared global cultural dreamscape. And yet, though most of them are still actively producing astounding imagery, the tools and techniques they use now are not at all the ones they started out with. These masters have also pioneered the very techniques that make movies the dazzling experience they are today.

Just as the age of sail gave way to steamships, and the horse-drawn carriage to the automobile, technology advances relentlessly. In our world what was once novel and bleeding-edge becomes the norm within a few years. Nowhere is this seen more clearly than in the visual-effects world.

I think back to when I was a young VFX practitioner in the early 1980s and compare it to where we are today. At that time we built physical miniatures and photographed them with cameras, which drove strips of light-sensitive film through mechanical movements as precisely machined as Swiss watches. Often we would take those images and combine them together using arcane optical printers that nevertheless often yielded jaw-dropping results. Think Douglas Trumbull's images for *Bladerunner* and *Close Encounters of the Third Kind*, or Richard Edlund's work on *Star Wars*, if you want to visualize that technique's golden age.

We used to paint matte paintings on glass, and combine them in the camera with live action or they would be combined later in the optical printer. Sometimes we would use forced-perspective techniques like foreground miniatures to extend sets. High-speed photography gave the models their correct movement so they would "scale." Blowing up models was my favorite part of the whole process, which is a measure of how much we were all really just kids in grown-up bodies getting paid to stay kids. Since wire removal—and all the other myriad of paint-out techniques—was still over the horizon, we had to keep the wires hidden, using the thinnest gauges of piano wire or monofilament possible to fly a spaceship or to lash an alien Queen's tail. There was front-screen and rear-screen "process" projection, both now obsolete, replaced by digital greenscreen compositing. Those massive projectors are now museum pieces, or for all I know being used to create artificial reefs. Not one of these techniques is still widely practiced. Cameras are digital now, with no moving parts except the lens elements and the fans that keep them cool. Film is arguably gone except for its use by a handful of filmmakers, none of them among the new generation. And certainly film is 100 percent gone for compositing. The optical printer itself has gone the way of the steam engine.

Though a small minority still clings to physical miniatures, the tide has overwhelmingly swept away the model shops with their buzzing Dremel-tools and the smell of resins, in favor of photo-realistic digital models. Physical miniatures have become a quaint artisanal niche, though still fondly remembered by those of us who started in that era, but nevertheless resoundingly obsolete. To bring a creature to life back then you had three choices: prosthetic makeup (or a rubber suit) on an actor, stop-motion animation, or an animatronic puppet moved by hydraulics or puppeteers. Stop motion is now gone, except for the occasional film that makes a virtue of the stylized look, and animatronics are in a slow sunset, now mostly phased out by computer animation.

Makeup is still very much with us, but its domain has been deeply eroded by the creation of photo-realistic, fully-expressive characters, such as Gollum, in *The Lord of the Rings* films, or the simians in the new *Planet of the Apes* movies, and the Na'vi characters done for my own *Avatar*—all three examples done by Joe Letteri's amazing team at Weta Digital in New Zealand. Now, instead of actors having to express emotion through uncomfortable and constricting layers of foam rubber, they can express freely while a Performance Capture system literally captures every nuance of their performance and stores it in the computer so that animators may apply that performance to the humanoid character the actor is playing. It's a whole new world.

About the only thing that's stayed the same in cinematography is that we still use light going through glass lenses to form an image on a recording substrate—even if that substrate is now an unmoving sensor as opposed to a racing strip of film—and even that domain is being relentlessly invaded by the creation of characters, sets, landscapes, whole worlds using computer modeling and animation. CG lighting has come to look as real as bouncing photons around in the physical world, and even the very definition of cinematography is changing, when increasingly large amounts of a movie are lit entirely virtually. But, as the French saying goes, the more things change the more they stay the same. Despite the almost complete replacement of every single trick and technique that effects wizards prided themselves on back then, in its essence, the job hasn't changed at all. The goal was always to bring worlds and characters out of the imagination and onto the screen by whatever means necessary. We learned the techniques that had been pioneered before us and we pioneered our own. It was that no-holds-barred pioneering spirit that drove the change that ultimately made obsolete everything we'd learned starting out.

The visual effects masters in this book all share in common that transition across the eras, from analog to digital. I consider them my contemporaries, since we are all about the same age, give or take 15 years. And we all, earlier or later in our careers, spanned the two sides of the uncanny valley. We started in a world of models, film cameras, and optical printers, and are now working away in the digital world happy as hogs in a waller. Most of the masters honored in this book made major contributions to advancing the art of computer animation and digital visual effects. You couldn't be a pioneer of the new way of making outlandish images without being an early adopter, and you couldn't be an early adopter without becoming a pioneer yourself. It was a positive feedback loop. Every project offered challenges that were in fact opportunities to push the techniques farther and faster. And it was all market driven. Because when audiences got their first look at CG creatures and characters that looked utterly real and yet were so impossible it defied their ability to guess how they were done—they wanted more. Three of the masters in this book (Dennis Muren, John Knoll, and John Bruno) were there with me on *The Abyss* in 1989 to create the first soft-surface CG character ever seen in a motion picture—the so-called "pseudopod" or what I always called the water weenie. Though the film itself wasn't a huge hit, the impact of the pseudopod scene was enormous. It was an impossible yet utterly real character unlike anything audiences had seen before.

This led to Dennis Muren and John Rosengrant creating the T-1000 liquid metal dude in *Terminator 2: Judgment Day*, then to Dennis Muren's group bringing dinosaurs to life in *Jurassic Park*. Three milestones of pioneering CG in the span of four years—each building on the lessons of the prior one. The T-1000 would not have been possible without the pseudopod, and the T-Rex and velociraptors would not have been possible without the socking and splining tools developed for the T-1000. This was a revolution taking place at warp speed, and when audiences saw it, they voted with their wallets. Studios began to realize the game was changing and that films driven by visual imagination were the most successful ones out there. The visual effects gurus reacted to this sea change by figuring out how to incorporate the new technology into their art. Phil Tippet did early stop-motion (actually "go-motion") tests for *Jurassic Park*, but when he saw that the dinosaurs he had imagined since he was a kid could be made to absolutely come alive with computer animation, he set up his own CG group and never looked back. John Rosengrant, working for Stan Winston at the time, saw compelling proof that the future was in CG when they worked with ILM to create the T-1000 in 1991. Stan promptly put in a CG animation group in 1992, the first makeup and prosthetics shop to have one. And to this day, John is a consummate character creator who unifies the fields of both physical and virtual drawing, and sculpting to design characters that may then be physically built, such as *Iron Man*, or exist only virtually, as with our creatures on *Avatar*.

The VFX world also quickly realized that before you create impossible images using just ones and zeroes, you had to have a rock-solid grasp of how light and motion worked in the real world. And all the gurus in this book, as they transitioned from the analog to the digital era, brought with them the nuts-and-bolts experience of real-world photography that they'd been practicing for years. They also brought with them the fundamentals of art—mood, perspective, composition, subtext, drama. The early days of CG were dominated by a reductionist philosophy that the real world could be broken down into mathematical rules—algorithms—which, if they were sophisticated enough, would inevitably produce an image on the screen indistinguishable from reality. But that ain't how it works. While there is some truth to the reductionist philosophy, it lacks a fundamental ingredient: the magic of the artist's eye. It takes an artist to see why the shot is not working, not a math major. In the brave new world of CG, both had to work together as a team. Many of the gurus herein are artists themselves, but all of them know how to lead a team of artists, also known as herding cats. Many of them are techies at heart, but all of them know how to lead a team of code-writers and engineers—also known as herding cats, but the cats are all younger and smarter than you are. And all of our featured wizards know how to get both left-brain and right-brain members of the team to work together.

Creating great visual effects is no longer about producing a few jaw-dropping shots. We had 42 CG shots of the liquid metal guy on *T2*. On *Avatar*, 15 years later, there were over 2000 CG character shots. Visual effects facilities have become massive engines for shot production, so more and more the job of the supervisor is about managing a pipeline—a vast and almost incomprehensible system by which money and dreams are fed into one end and shots pour out the other. To do this requires the creation of a culture—both a culture for the facility, and a culture for each movie project—and these cultures are, to a large degree, an extension of the philosophy and personality of the effects supervisor. With so many people working on a single film, the VFX supervisor must find the balance of controlling the process, to protect the facility's profit margin and shot quality—but they must also empower people to express themselves and solve problems. The VFX supervisor is the morale officer, in charge of keeping the channels of communication clear, not only within the facility, but also with the filmmaker whose vision they are bringing to life. It's a group dynamic, and when it works well, it can be the most rewarding experience possible—to be part of something monumental and magical, history-making and record-breaking.

VFX is a love affair with the impossible. The magicians in this book are driven by the desire to dazzle. Like any good magician, they know the trick but will never reveal it—at least never all of it. Otherwise, they think, anybody could do it. But that's not really true, because you can know all the technique in the world and still not be a visual effects master. The master must know which technique to use, and when, and must have the vision and perseverance to realize an impossible image that never existed before except in the imagination. Together, and with many others, these masters pioneered the world of image creation we now inhabit. It's a world in which nothing is impossible, any image that can be conceived can be realized, and the only limitation is our imagination. **James Cameron**

Foreword > by Lorenzo di Bonaventura

Prolific blockbuster and quality genre-film producer

Not possible. Possible. Not possible. Possible. Not possible...Possible! Pushing the boundaries beyond what's known is, in my experience, one of the most exciting aspects of VFX. I've had a front-row seat watching Scott Farrar make a Transformer metamorphose in the most spectacular, ever-impossibly complex ways; Stefen Fangmeier conjure angry oceans and a wave exceeding your imagination for *The Perfect Storm*; and John Gaeta help Keanu Reeves first dodge, then stop bullets in *The Matrix*. It's thrilling work that can define how the audience first experiences and, later remembers the sensation and emotion of that first exposure.

The artists celebrated in this book are truly that: artists. Yet, often, they are simply thought of as the computer-savvy guys who merely push a computer to greater heights. Or perhaps this is a notion of the recent past, and this book recognizes that this misunderstanding has begun to disappear. I know that was my journey with VFX. Now that I have participated in more than 150 films in one way or another, I've learned why what these masters do is so much more. Storytelling is such an immense aspect of VFX. Yes, effects are often meant to make you go "Wow," but they also shape a film in so many other ways. With 3D creatures, VFX artists help imbue characters with personality: it's why you can fall in love with them or believe their ability to menace and destroy. Of course one can't diminish the roles of the writer and director, but during the transition from the page to the shoot and finally to execution of the VFX, the nuances and colorfulness of a character are born from a great artistic VFX collaborator. When Scott and his team, working with Michael Bay on *Transformers*, make you love Bumblebee, it's not about how cool his transformations are—it's about how his body posture, his eye movement and more contribute to your response.

Relying on VFX for storytelling is not a new idea. I remember sitting in the front row of a theater in Brookline, Massachusetts, watching the opening salvo of *Star Wars*, with the battleship drifting overhead. I immediately knew that we had entered a brand new world. Yet, over the last 25 years I've been in this business, we increasingly have demanded more of VFX to establish new worlds, carry characterization further, and blow boundaries in execution. In the movies I have worked on, we have taken audiences to the moon, inside a computer, through a wormhole, through a monster hurricane, and on other epic journeys. These were all visual extravaganzas, and they all relied on the staggering imagination and execution of the effects to make movie-goers believe that the story they were being told was "real." But when these fabulous images can also evoke a whole new dimension with a single shot, it gives the filmmakers the capacity to tell a larger story. It also leaves an indelible imprint that will last well past the initial viewing.

What is often overlooked is how to make things feel part of the real world or to hide the unreal by the high quality of the execution. For the movie *Red*, Bruce Willis had a great idea: Let's take a familiar action-movie sequence—a cop throwing open his car door, then jumping out of the car with his gun held high and firing—and let it unfold in a subtle yet ultimately quite different fashion. His idea was to have his character exit the car while it was still moving and, without losing his balance, fire away. To top it off, the creative team decided the car's bumper should slide by his leg in a way that would make the audience expect he'd be hit and then, miraculously, it just brushes by his pant leg. Physically, it's not possible to pull this off, so our VFX wiz James Madigan worked his magic to render the fantasy-physics aspect of it undetectable. Without those effects, the gag wouldn't have worked. Among the VFX creators in this book are some of the early pioneering giants and some of the current masters of the craft. This book could feature many more of the talented men and women who are considered the industry's finest, but the work of this group represents an awesome array. Myself, I look forward to being inspired by the many VFX journeys to come and to being surprised by what indeed is possible. Enjoy *Masters of FX*! **Lorenzo di Bonaventura**

Introduction > The Masters of **FX**

A spaceship zooms over the audience's head. A tyrannosaurus chasing down a jeep incites screams in the theater. A tiger wins the hearts of viewers by learning to get along with a young boy in the middle of the ocean. These are some of the most remarkable film images from recent times, ushered to the screen thanks to talented visual and special effects supervisors.

Visual and special effects supervisors are the magicians of the film world, seemingly conjuring impossible imagery onto our movie screens. Both artist and technician, an effects supervisor must have a firm grasp of film language, photography, and—increasingly commonly—computer graphics. However, special effects (generally be completed on set) and visual effects (generally done in post-production), are surprisingly not new. Some of the earliest films relied on trick effects photography. As movies began to showcase more intricate storylines, more characters, and more locations, special and visual effects were used to broaden the scope—firstly via in-camera, practical, and optical techniques, then with a thunderous new wave of digital imagery. Of course, many of the most ingenious shots in filmmaking history are ones still completed as "in-camera" stunts.

With so many productions now requiring special and visual effects—an alien creature, a helicopter crash, a surging ocean, or even just the view outside a car window—the role of the effects supervisor is critical. Their job often encompasses many facets, from planning shots and sequences that execute a specific idea in the script, to co-ordinating on-set action, and then sometimes leading an army of effects artists working together to bring a director's vision to the screen.

Masters of FX traces the individual stories of 16 visual and special effects supervisors—many of whom are multiple Academy Award winners—with personal on-set and post-production tales. The artists profiled include those who began in the practical and optical effects worlds of effects, as well as those who have perfected the art of on-set special effects and miniatures. The supervisors in this book have directly experienced and embraced the trend toward the digital realm, where incredible software solutions and computing power help bring photorealistic worlds and creatures to the screen.

As the following pages reveal, it is clear that each supervisor profiled is a master problem solver. Indeed that is often the nature of their role in the making of a film—to think quickly, but be confident about their ideas, a task sometimes made more difficult when new techniques or technologies must be developed to make certain effects possible.

John Bruno examines his close association with director James Cameron on films such as *The Abyss* and *True Lies*, and how retaining a strong sense of practical and in-camera effects is extremely important in the digital era.

Chris Corbould, a veteran of numerous Bond films, as well as Christopher Nolan's *Batman* trilogy and *Inception*, discusses his on-set experiences as a special effects supervisor.

Richard Edlund, who worked on the original *Star Wars* films, speaks of practical ingenuity in the final scenes of *Raiders of the Lost Ark*, as well as getting the Marshmallow Man in *Ghostbusters* to roam New York.

Scott Farrar imparts his filmmaking knowledge from the futuristic *Minority Report* to the shape-shifting metallic robots of the *Transformers* films.

Paul Franklin traces his steps in creating a brand new visual effects company and forging a strong relationship with Christopher Nolan to work on the director's *The Dark Knight* trilogy, *Inception*, and *Interstellar*.

Karen Goulekas recounts her experiences on several disaster blockbusters, including *The Day After Tomorrow*, with particular insight into following a passion for art and filmmaking.

Ian Hunter discusses his approach to miniature effects in films, including *The Dark Knight* and *Inception*, with tips on building models and blowing them up.

John Knoll, co-inventor of Photoshop, explores the projection mapping advancements made in *Star Wars:*

[1] Effects artists from Industrial Light & Magic (ILM) capture blasts on a scale model of the Death Star surface in **Star Wars: Episode IV—A New Hope**. Several visual effects supervisors featured in this book worked on the watershed effects in this film and its sequels.

[2] Richard Parker from **Life of Pi**. Real-life references and detailed anatomic and animation studies of tigers helped the effects artists create a stunningly photorealistic performance.

Episode I—The Phantom Menace and on-set motion capture enabling the character of Davy Jones in the *Pirates of the Caribbean* series.

Robert Legato discusses his collaborations with Cameron on *Titanic*, where models, CG water, and motion-captured actors were combined, as well as films such as *The Aviator* and *Hugo*, which he completed with Martin Scorsese.

Joe Letteri has embraced high frame rates— most recently in *The Hobbit*—as well as pushing the envelope of performance capture in *The Lord of the Rings* trilogy, *Avatar*, and the recent *Planet of the Apes* reboots.

Dennis Muren details his journey at Industrial Light & Magic, from the analog world of *Star Wars: Episodes IV–VI*, through to computer-graphics breakthroughs with the liquid-metal T-1000 in *Terminator 2: Judgment Day* and the realistic dinosaurs of *Jurassic Park*.

John Rosengrant reveals the secrets behind key practical, animatronic, and makeup effects gags for the Terminators in *Terminator 2: Judgment Day* and the dinosaurs in *Jurassic Park*.

Phil Tippett also devolves information on his creature work, having moved from the stop-frame animation of *The Empire Strikes Back*'s Tauntans and AT-ATs to the frightening CGI bugs of *Starship Troopers*.

Doug Trumbull has worked on perhaps some of the most defining visual effects films in modern memory with *2001: A Space Odyssey*, *Close Encounters of the Third Kind*, and *Blade Runner*, and continues to champion the use of high frame rates and immersive cinema.

Bill Westenhofer outlines his path to making firstly talking animals and then provides his master class in the critical components of completely photorealistic creatures, such as the tiger, Richard Parker, in *Life of Pi*.

Edson Williams showcases the art of beauty work and digital skin grafting, techniques that rejuvenated Brad Pitt in *The Curious Case of Benjamin Button* and made "Skinny Steve" in the *Captain America* films.

The artists in *Masters of FX* highlight just some of their special and visual effects credits, providing practical examples of how famous effects shots were achieved. Moreover, they give insight into the skills necessary to become an effects supervisor and reveal how important the process of making observations of the real world are in bringing final shots to the screen. If you've ever wondered "how did they do that?" then here's your chance to go behind the scenes with the minds behind the magic.

1 > John Bruno

John Bruno had established himself as an animator, layout artist, and story director when he saw George Lucas' original *Star Wars* in 1977. "I thought, 'Man, what do I have to do to do realistic effects like that? The simplest thing like the lightsabers were just such a visual treat and I didn't know how they were done." Still pondering a career in visual effects, Bruno met effects supervisor Richard Edlund while working on *Heavy Metal* in Montreal. Richard was giving a talk to the Canadian Film Commission about the 1980 release, *The Empire Strikes Back.* "I attended that seminar and introduced myself to him. I said something silly like 'I really want to do what you do.' I was doing a lot of complicated classic animation for a film called *Heavy Metal*. And there were a lot of things that applied directly to live-action special effects."

"Later that year," adds Bruno, "I heard that Richard was looking for somebody to do animated effects on Steven Spielberg's *Poltergeist*. I brought an effects reel from *Heavy Metal* to show him at MGM, where Richard was applying the final finishing touches to *Raiders of the Lost Ark*. The ghosts in *Raiders of the Lost Ark* were done with cloth moving in a water tank. "He wanted better control for *Poltergeist*," says Bruno, "and suggested that I come up to San Rafael, to ILM, and set up an animation department to do ectoplasm and other animated effects. I was just in heaven at ILM. Our department did *Poltergeist*, *E.T.*, *Star Trek II*, and *Return of the Jedi*."

When Edlund left ILM to form Boss Film, Bruno went with him and would contribute to films such as *Poltergeist II: The Other Side*, *Batman Returns*, *Ghostbusters*, and *Cliffhanger*. He then branched out as a freelancer visual effects supervisor, soon forming an on-going relationship with director James Cameron. The two first collaborated on *The Abyss*, a film that saw one of the first CG creatures ever photographically realized on film—the water pseudopod.

ILM had been crucial in showing Bruno the possibilities of CG. "In the early 1980s, Sprocket Systems, an ILM subsidiary, was creating incredible imagery with CG," he recalls. "They really helped me understand 3D animation and lighting volumes. On my way to lunch one day, George Lucas asked Mike Pangrazio and I to go next door to Sprocket Systems and talk to Alvy Ray Smith and learn what we could about computer animation. It was just the most amazing thing I ever experienced. We were shown the 'Genesis effect' for *Star Trek II*, which was my introduction to the world of 3D. It had wire-frame animation of a planet and how to move it and light it. I was shown how to take a flat surface and pin it to a globe, rotate it, and light it. If the flat surface was water, you could roll it into the shape of a tube and it would animate in three dimensions. I remembered that. That's how the water pseudopod from *The Abyss* eventually came into being."

Bruno next helped design effects for Cameron's *Terminator 2: Judgment Day*, then supervised effects for *True Lies*, and later designed shots and the shooting methodology for *Titanic*. "I made two dives in Mir 2, to the Titanic wreck myself," says Bruno, referring to an expedition with the director in 1995. Photography of the wreck and its exploration would be used in the final narrative. When Universal Pictures offered Bruno the feature film *Virus* to direct, Rob Legato took over visual effects supervision duties on *Titanic*.

Bruno would later work again with Cameron co-directing (with Stan Winston) *Terminator 2 3-D: Battle Across Time*, for the Universal Studios Theme Parks and again on *Avatar*—coming on during effects production to work with Weta Digital and other vendors on several key sequences. "I did a number of training sequences, with Neytiri teaching Avatar Jake Sully to hunt," says Bruno.

[1] John Bruno with the "Terror Dog" puppet from **Ghostbusters**.

[2] Two mutants, played by Shawn Ashmore and Aaron Stanford, battle it out using fire and ice effects in **X-Men: The Last Stand**.

The visual effects supervisor's other credits include *AVP: Alien vs. Predator*, *X-Men: The Last Stand*, *Rush Hour 3*, *The Twilight Saga: Breaking Dawn—Parts 1 and 2*, and *Hercules*. Bruno also re-teamed with Cameron as expedition director for the documentary, *Deepsea Challenge 3D*, which followed the director's successful 2012 dive in a custom-made submersible to the deepest point on the planet.

Ghostbusters

Bruno was able to draw on his rich experience in animation and camera effects skills to work with effects supervisor Richard Edlund on Ivan Reitman's *Ghostbusters* (1984). Three sequences were stand-outs for Bruno—the final blowing up of the Gozer temple atop Central Park West; the creation of the green ghost known as Onion Head; and Mr Stay Puft, the Marshmallow Man.

Onion Head and the Marshmallow Man would become the most enduring characters from *Ghostbusters*. "In discussing the 'Onion Head' I had a long conversation with Dan Akroyd, who said it was supposed to be (his friend) John Belushi," notes Bruno. "He said the best way to think about that character was Bluto from *Animal House*—he was a slob. Always. A disgusting blob."

"He was supposed to be floating three to four feet off the ground," adds Bruno. "The character was created by a performer, Mark Bryan Wilson, wearing a foam rubber suit that was painted lime-green and filmed in front of black cloth. No blue screen or green screen. Mark's

legs were wrapped in black duvateen so you couldn't see them, and the suit rested above his waist. His mouth and eyes were operated by puppeteers dressed in black, sitting below and behind him. Someone else's arm operated the tongue. The camera was locked off and we would move 'Slimer' around according to the shot. To make him look hyper-kinetic we shot the footage at six frames a second. It was just such crazy footage that in dailies we'd be laughing our asses off."

The Marshmallow Man was also a man in a latex suit, played by Bill Bryan. "He was six-feet tall, his face, eyes, and brow were cable actuated from under a set built to replicate Central Park West," explains Bruno. "As Mr Stay Puft walked, cables from his right leg ran through the set—along a slot—to a trolley with three puppeteers aboard that were pulled along as the character trundled up the street. We filmed all of the action at 72 frames per second to add weight and scale. The police cars, fire trucks, and taxi cabs were all made from Revel model car kits and were moved with fishing line."

[1] Clouds form atop the Central Park West building as supernatural events take hold in New York City.

[1]

[2] John Bruno (far left) examines the Onion Head puppet used in **Ghostbusters**.

The Gozer temple explosions were realized using a miniature building. The top of the building only existed in miniature, built to scale to match a building on Central Park West. Optically composited cloud tank footage, scaled explosions, animated effects, and matte-painted backgrounds completed these illusions. "Those shots looked amazing, especially the wide shot at the end when the clouds go away and vaporize over the city, but they really came down to the wire," remembers Bruno. "At the machine shop at Boss Film, Richard Edlund designed and had built a high-speed 65mm camera so we could actually film the destruction of the 112.5-foot tall Marshmallow Man. We also had to build a 65mm to 35mm reduction optical printer. Both of these pieces of equipment were in the works while we were filming, with only ten months to the release date."

"I can actually recall today the Gozer temple shot numbers—GT73 and GT76," adds Bruno. "We had to be finished on a Sunday. I'd walked into Boss Film, all the lights were on, and over the loudspeakers Jimi Hendrix's *Purple Haze* was playing really loud. I walked into the optical department and the doors were open—they're never open because the room has a vacuum-sealed entrance for dust. I could hear the 65mm optical printer running. There was an empty bottle of Jack Daniels lying on its side and next to the printer was a big pile of metal shavings. The mechanism for the printer was worn to a stub so it was grinding metal to metal. On a couch upstairs was our optical printer artist. He said, 'Bruno, GT73 and GT76 are finished!' And then he fell back to sleep. That was just two weeks before the film was released."

The Abyss

One of the common questions asked of visual effects supervisors is "how are we going to do this effect?" That challenge was presented by James Cameron to Bruno for the water tentacle creature in the director's deep-sea oil-rig adventure *The Abyss* (1989). "This pseudopod, as we called it," says Bruno, "was a 'sea water' probe controlled by an alien force. It had to move and react with sensitivity to its surroundings and finally communicate by morphing into the image of the person confronting it—it had to take the form of the actors' faces."

"I was trying to work out how it could be done," continues Bruno. "For *Poltergeist* we had a scene where Carol Anne was drawn to a TV. The screen distorts into a hand that streaks past her into the back wall of the bedroom. To do this we stop-motioned 26 acrylic hands that morphed into back-lit cell animation. I didn't really think something like that would work. We built acrylic sculpts of the pseudopod and stop-motion replacement animation was a possibility, but a distant one."

The storyboarded sequence was sent out for bidding to various visual effects studios. "Then," says Bruno, "Industrial Light & Magic showed us a test. Something they'd animated looked like it could work, but nobody was 100 per cent certain. If anybody could do it, we thought it would be ILM. They had the background and the skills. In blind trust we awarded the job to them!'"

At ILM, the team—including visual effects supervisor Dennis Muren, Mark Dippe, Lincoln Hu, Steve Williams, and John Knoll—would devise the methodology for bringing the water tentacle to life. To help guide the artists with a suitable look for the pseudopod, Bruno sent a rough template. "We took the background plates and we animated where the water tentacle was moving in the completed sequence," he says.

It was also the beginning of digital compositing that promised enhanced integration of computer-generated imagery. "Dennis Muren would rely on nascent computer animation and rendering software to realize the movement and appearance of the pseudopod," notes Bruno. "ILM created a surface water program that was an early version of RenderMan. It looked like water.

It looked like the surface of the ocean and it would animate and undulate. If you took something like that and wrapped it around a wire-frame tube, that was—in theory—the water tentacle."

Bruno says that ILM also had to expand its proprietary morphing process to allow the photorealistic morphing of the character's faces to the end of the water tentacle. This, and further improvements to the studio's CG pipeline, would inform later work on James Cameron's *Terminator 2: Judgment Day* (1991), a film that Bruno also designed visual effects for. "Actually, the original look of the water tentacle—before it was made to look more water-like and transparent—was liquid mercury," recalls Bruno. "On *Terminator 2*, Jim [Cameron] actually wanted a reflective chrome character for the T-1000 policeman, especially for that shot of him pouring himself into the left seat of a flying helicopter and telling the pilot to get out."

Ultimately, *The Abyss* would become a milestone film in the history of visual effects films—partly for its CG water tentacle, but also due to the multi-vendor approach Bruno adopted in completing the film's

[1] The pseudopod takes shape in wire frame and final rendered forms in computer-screen captures from Industrial Light & Magic. (Photo © AF archive / Alamy)

[2] The pseudopod takes the form of actress Mary Elizabeth Mastrantonio. ILM had to solve several computer graphics problems to enable the water creature, including facial scan and morphing techniques for this scene.

[3] In addition to computer graphics, miniatures, and special effects, much of **The Abyss** was filmed at the abandoned Cherokee Nuclear Power Plant outside Gaffney, South Carolina, which was converted into a massive water tank for the underwater scenes.

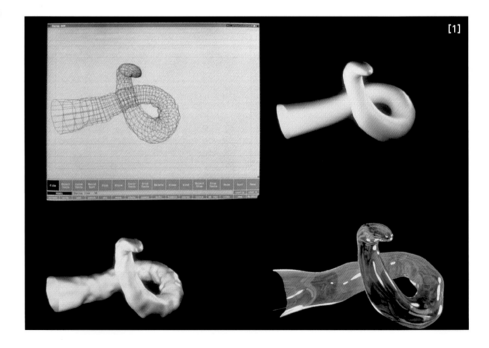

[1]

complicated water, miniature, stop motion, digital, and optical effects. "Before *The Abyss*," he says, "one facility handled all the work for a film. But *The Abyss* was the first time effects were distributed between multiple vendors. We had different companies working on different effects. We had a giant 60-feet long model submarine set, with an overhead gantry crane with hanging, marionetted Cab One and Flatbed miniatures. I'd even taken a 42-foot model of the Benthic Explorer out into the open ocean in Gray's Bay, Washington, in eight-to-ten foot seas to film it in a squall. It all seems crazy now! We tried to get as much as possible in-camera, but most people remember the first time they saw the water tentacle—that took everybody by surprise. And the kudos for that should go to Dennis Muren, John Knoll, and animator Steve Williams."

True Lies

Cameron's *True Lies* (1994), featuring actor Arnold Schwarzenegger as a spy who must rescue his own family, again saw the director look to Bruno for both practical and digital effects solutions. That was particularly the case for the climactic Harrier jet sequence in which Schwarzenegger's character flies the jet to the top of a Florida office building, shoots out the 30th floor, fights off a terrorist, and retrieves his daughter.

"Our theory for that scene was to get as much in-camera as possible," says Bruno. "Meaning, if we could make that jet fly, for real, with Arnold in it, we should do it. No one to that date had done a photorealistic digital airplane, so digital wasn't really an option. There was going to be a lot of human interaction required, including a fist fight on the jet. I had just done *Cliffhanger*, which had a lot of practical effects where the actors fought on a crashed helicopter that hung from the side of the cliff in Northern Italy, so I knew having something there for the actors to interact with was going to add realism and was the right way to go."

Cameron was easily convinced, but Bruno still had to conceive how certain shots would be accomplished practically, and most importantly, safely. "I thought, if we made a full-sized cockpit and wing section and we were high enough in the air, we could film our characters in-camera," says Bruno. "With the cockpit on a platform on a high-rise building or parking lot, maybe close-ups could be in-camera meaning fewer VFX shots. Then it was suggested that we make a full-sized Harrier jet mock up and put that on top of a building or a parking structure in Miami. The Brickell Building was chosen. We'd be able to shoot there with the characters on the mock-up jet attached to a hydraulic gimbaled motion base. With the jet on the motion base, and using a crane, we could film the actors flying and fighting on the back of the jet, while in the distance we could see downtown Miami. All of this in-camera."

During shooting on the roof of the Brickell Building, Cameron requested that the jet be filmed lifting off with Arnold shown flying it. "We could have filmed some of

[1] James Cameron on the special effects set of **True Lies**. A model jet fighter used to film part of the Harrier sequence is behind him.

[2] Arnold Schwarzenegger in the Harrier cockpit. The special effects and stunts teams were crucial to making the Harrier shots possible. This included the development of a marionette rig on a crane that would lift the Harrier as the jet launched, and later for when it was seen hovering. The visual effects team digitally removed the wires in post-production.

this green screen," says Bruno, "but I really thought maybe we could get a couple of shots if we lifted the plane off the motion base on the roof and then moved the camera around it. I talked to the special effects supervisor Tommy Fisher to see if it was possible to do that. Tommy said, 'Sure, I'll swing it over the street with two-inch cable tied to it!' I went to the crane operator and asked the same question. The mock-up jet weighs 7,000 pounds and he told me the crane was rated for 10,000. After getting approval from Joel Kramer, the stunt coordinator, we set that plan into motion!"

"We ran wires from the wingtips to a couple of buildings," continues Bruno, "so that we could turn the

plane left or right. We had stunt actors 350 feet above Brickell Ave. Jim circled in a camera helicopter and filmed the action, giving the jet the illusion of movement."

When the jet landed on the street at the end of the sequence, Arnold Schwarzenegger and actress Eliza Dushku were actually in the jet as it was lowered by crane from 50 feet and gently touched down bumping into a parked police car. "We later composited fan blades into the jet intakes and animated jet exhaust," says Bruno. "People don't know how we did that to this day! And when I think about it, it was pretty crazy."

X-Men: The Last Stand

Brett Ratner's *X-Men: The Last Stand* (2006) called for more problem solving. "We had two major sequences I remember that we had to approach differently," recalls Bruno. "The first was the Professor Charles Xavier (Patrick Stewart) and Erik Lehnsherr (Ian McKellen) rejuvenation shots, which ended up being so expertly handled by Lola VFX. The goal was to make the actors appear 25 years younger—a technique used for the first time in this film. Then there was the Golden Gate Bridge sequence, where Magneto moves the bridge from it's current location across San Francisco Bay to Alcatraz."

In the film, Magneto was to use his magnetic powers to relocate the Golden Gate Bridge to Alcatraz where a mutant processing facility is located that Magneto wants to destroy. "I came up with the concepts for this sequence early in the production," notes Bruno. "I thought we should build a full sized, 1:1 section of the bridge, some 300-feet long and 90-feet wide on a parking lot, then build the railings, put a greenscreen around it, and do most of the action in camera—the cars driving at 35mph, people running, cars crashing. Then we would just have to extend the backgrounds. The studio, Edward Verreaux (the production designer), and Brett Ratner all went for it!"

The bridge sequence would also be achieved through the use of CG and very large miniatures. "When Magneto moves the bridge off its foundations and flies it over the Bay to Alcatraz, that's a combination of large miniatures and CG effects composited into live-action background plates," says Bruno. "We used a large bridge miniature—measuring 10-feet wide and 60-feet long—for close-up pieces, and for shots as it swings across camera and crashes to the ground."

Part of the reason behind these very practical choices for the bridge sequence—apart from Bruno's view that they helped ground the shots in reality—was time. "Trying to get things in-camera speeds up your time for completing shots," he says. "The fewer shots you have

[1] Jean Grey (Famke Janssen) atomizes Professor Xavier (Patrick Stewart). The final shot involved digitizing real objects in the scene, such as chairs, books, and lamps, and then turning them into dust.

[2] The Golden Gate Bridge, under the control of Magneto, slides to a new location in San Francisco.

to complete digitally speeds up your delivery schedule. We literally only had 12 months to do the entire film—we started April 15th and we finished April 28th, which was the final delivery of the last shot of the film."

Other key effects in the film included Angel's escape and flight from his father's high-rise office. This was a practical effect, with the actor flown across an intersection and over a church. Artists then painted out the cables and added his wings.

Further shots were required for Storm's monumental weather creations, Juggernaut's destructive powers, and the atomization powers wrought by Jean Grey as she transforms into Phoenix causing gravity to reverse and emptying San Francisco Bay.

X-Men: The Last Stand was Bruno's first collaboration with Ratner, but they would work together again on *Rush Hour 3*, *Tower Heist*, and *Hercules*.

2 > Chris Corbould

Chris Corbould has worked on such incredible effects as the tank chase in *GoldenEye* and the Batmobiles in *The Dark Knight* trilogy. However, his introduction to the world of effects was much more auspicious (although not short on exposure to film stars and celebrities). It began on Ken Russell's 1975 film, *Tommy*, about a disabled boy who becomes a master pinball player. The film starred Eric Clapton, Tina Turner, Oliver Reed, Ann-Margret, and The Who. "My uncle, Colin Chilvers, was the special effects supervisor on the film," says Corbould, "and he phoned me one day whilst I was on my school summer break and asked me if I wanted to help him for a couple of weeks. Being a massive The Who fan, I jumped at the chance, not realizing that it would determine my career for the next 40 years."

Corbould's first job on *Tommy* was to open hundreds of tins of baked beans for a scene in which Ann-Margret's character is kneeling in front of a television, when suddenly the screen explodes with baked beans. "This effect was achieved by constructing a chute behind the TV wall," explains Corbould, "and then tipping five one-hundred gallon tanks simultaneously down the chute and funneling them out through the narrow TV screen."

"The rush of baked beans," he adds, "sent Ann-Margret slithering across the set where she commenced to writhe around in a rhythmic dance. Ken Russell loved the shot and we finished the day doing more takes of Ann dancing. We needed to do some more shots on Monday, after the weekend, but upon arriving on Monday morning, the baked beans had started to bubble and ferment over the weekend, giving off a less-than-pleasant smell. Ann-Margret, a true professional, carried on the scene until completion."

Corbould would continue on *Tommy* for a number of weeks, helping to film sequences with performers such as Tina Turner and Elton John. "This event changed my whole perspective on life," he says. "I never went back to school but obtained a trainee post at an SFX company in Pinewood called Effects Associates where I commenced an eight year learning period on engineering, hydraulics, pneumatics, and all aspects of special effects." After this time, Corbould contributed to the Bond films *The Spy Who Loved Me* and *Moonraker*, plus *Superman*, *Superman II*, and *Superman III*.

His first film in the role of overall special effects supervisor was *GoldenEye*, and Corbould's technical and artistic prowess has been on show in every Bond film made since, as well as major action films such as *Firestorm*, *The Mummy*, *Lara Croft: Tomb Raider*, *X-Men: First Class*, and *John Carter*. Corbould has also become a frequent collaborator with director Christopher Nolan.

As a special effects supervisor, Corbould is responsible for practical and in-camera effects that are often captured at the time of principal photography. These effects range from props, mechanized vehicles, atmospheric effects (such as rain and fire), and the use of miniatures. Corbould's most well-known effects contributions include the *GoldenEye* tank chase, the ice lake pursuit in *Die Another Day*, the digger scene and train crash in *Skyfall*, the vehicles in *The Dark Knight* trilogy, and the rotating sets featured in *Inception*'s dreamscape sequences.

Despite 40 years of experience, Corbould says he still dreams about an effects shot "many times over in my sleep prior to actually filming the real thing. The sets are sometimes extremely expensive and failure would mean massive rebuilds, delay, and cost." He notes that on all these films, the "spectacular events" are a collaboration between special effects, stunts, construction, visual effects, and many other departments. "On a personal level," says Corbould, "I have nothing but admiration and respect for the dedicated effects crew that have worked with me over the years."

[1] Chris Corbould attends the world premiere of **Skyfall** in the UK.

[2] Chris Corbould sits in front of a practical robot built for **Lara Croft: Tomb Raider**.

GoldenEye

Martin Campbell's *GoldenEye* (1995) would be a pivotal film for Corbould. Not only did it give him his first experience as the overall special effects supervisor on a major action film, but it also started a stellar run of James Bond films.

Of all the physical effects in the film, one standout scene is the Russian tank chase through the streets of St Petersburg. "The tank chase had an interesting start to its life." recalls Corbould. "I was called to the office of Martin Campbell, who was seated at a table with (producers) Barbara Broccoli and Michael Wilson. In the script was a motorbike chase. Martin was concerned it was not very original and asked me if I had any ideas how to make it better. I thought for a second and then said, 'Get rid of the motorbike and let Bond steal a tank from the military camp where he was.' Hence the tank chase was born."

Corbould's next responsibility was to acquire the appropriate tanks for the job. "Weirdly enough," he says, "I managed to obtain two Russian T54 tanks from different sources in the UK. As they looked quite dated we decided to dress them up to look like T80 tanks, a more modern version. This included cutting a dummy driver's hatch in the body so that we could have Bond (Pierce Brosnan) look like he is driving the tank whilst in reality it was a hidden stunt driver, Gary Powell—who is himself now stunt coordinator on the current Bond films."

Further modifications were made to the tanks when it was determined that they might damage the road surfaces. The tanks were made lighter and fitted with dummy rotating tracks and tank dressing on top of a wheeled light armored carrier.

The stunt department, headed by Simon Crane, then tested the abilities of the tanks by driving over cars and

[1] A close-up view of the tank gun firing is captured on film. Scenes were shot over six weeks, partly on location in Russia as well as on dressed sets at Leavesden Studios in the UK.

[1]

[2] James Bond (Pierce Brosnan) commandeers a Russian tank. Corbould re-purposed actual tanks for the sequence, generally making them lighter and more maneuverable for filming.

through walls. Corbould suggests that little rigging was necessary on such walls since, he notes, "28 tons moving at 30mph pretty much goes through anything."

However, Corbould says, "we did have to rig a large articulated truck loaded with Perrier cans for the tank to split in two and also an ingenious contraption to capture a statue on its turret, which basically consisted of a loop of strong wire hanging down from the horse statue that lassoed the gun barrel of the tank as it drove through the fake stone plinth underneath it. We planned the sequence based on the fact that the car had to stick to traditional streets whereas the tank could take short cuts through walls."

"I think the most spectacular scene with the tank," adds Corbould, "was when it first appeared jumping through a high brick wall and landing in the road behind the car that it was pursuing. The stunt team had to time the jump to perfection as the tank took 200 yards to get up to speed and the car had to turn the corner at exactly the right moment. It was a great shot."

Die Another Day

Corbould orchestrated a vehicular chase of a different kind in Lee Tamahori's *Die Another Day* (2002) when he was asked to help stage a showdown on an ice lake in Iceland. "I remember a meeting in Pinewood Studios with Lee Tamahori, Barbara Broccoli, Michael Wilson, production designer Peter Lamont, and second unit director and stunt coordinator Vic Armstrong," recounts Corbould. "After a short conversation, Vic and I agreed that we should use the four-wheel drive versions of both the Aston Martin Vanquish and the Jaguar XKR to give the stunt drivers maximum control on the ice lake. This seemed a good idea at the time until I visited both car manufacturers and was told that there was no four-wheel drive version of either car. This posed a question: 'Do we try and convert standard production line Astons and Jaguars to four-wheel drive?'"

That's exactly what Corbould and his team did. With senior car engineer Andy Smith, Corbould engaged several technicians to completely change the engine, gearbox, and steering of four Aston Martins and four Jaguar XKRs. "We also had the job of designing and fabricating the weapons that were to be a large part of the chase," adds Corbould. "The Aston Martin possessed a missile rack in the front grill, motion sensing shotguns in the bonnet, and an ejector seat that would be used in the film to put the car back onto its wheels after being blown onto its roof by an explosion. It also had the ability to become invisible, although that capability was beyond my SFX team (and not one I was particularly a fan of)."

Meanwhile, the Jaguar required forward-facing rockets, rear-firing mines that came from the trunk, and a rotating mini gun that rose from the bodywork behind the driver. "Both cars also had a gadget that was totally practical and potentially life saving," notes Corbould. "As the cars were going to be racing on a real ice lake, I couldn't ignore the fact that there was the potential for the cars to go through the ice. We decided to fit automatically triggered inflation bags that would inflate when they came into contact with water, concealing them in pop-out panels on the bodywork."

On location in Iceland, safety teams would monitor the condition of the ice for signs of cracking. "The crew was all issued with heat retaining immersion suits as contact with the icy water—should they fall in—would normally only give you seconds to react," explains Corbould. "The person I really had sympathy with was George Cottle who was doubling Zao (Rick Yune) in the open-top Jaguar with a bald head."

"As we progressed through the sequence," continues Corbould, "it became apparent that the ice was starting to thaw and it became a race against time to get all the necessary action completed in time. Vic Armstrong achieved this the day before the safety team shut down the ice. The ice chase was a thrilling, demanding, and fulfilling experience that I believe produced one of the most unique car sequences on film."

[1] The modified, four-wheel drive Jaguar XKR and Aston Martin Vanquish on an Iceland ice lake. As the chase was filmed, inspectors would ensure that the ice was structurally sound for the vehicles to continue.

The Dark Knight trilogy

With *Batman Begins* (2005), *The Dark Knight* (2008), and *The Dark Knight Rises* (2012), Corbould would become synonymous with Batman vehicles, in particular the Batmobile and the Batpod.

The Batmobile—or Tumbler, as it became known—was envisaged by production designer, Nathan Crowley, as a vehicle with large double rear wheels, hydraulic flaps, jet propulsion, and a unique steering mechanism where the wheels were turned from side wings, rather than a central axle.

Basing their work on small mock ups and a full size polystyrene model of the Batmobile, Corbould's team began producing the unorthodox vehicle's features. "Within three to four months we had a skeletal running car ready to take out on a test track for initial trials at Longcross Studios," says Corbould, who notes that further tests also ensured the Batmobile could jump from ramps, eventually performing a 60-foot ramp jump while filming in Chicago.

Vehicle expert Andy Smith incorporated a 350 Chevrolet engine into the Batmobile—four shooting cars and a publicity car were built in total for *Batman Begins*. Stunt driver George Cottle developed a unique style of driving for it too, as Corbould explains: "This was derived from the fact that the windscreen consisted of a tiny triangle of tinted glass against which George would press his nose to get maximum vision."

Corbould followed up the Batmobile with the appearance of the Batpod in *The Dark Knight*, a film for which the supervisor earned an Academy Award nomination for achievement in visual effects. "When I first set eyes on the Batpod I thought that we were mad to even attempt to make it, but this was what Chris Nolan wanted," says Corbould. "My biggest immediate concern was the 20-inch wide front and back tires; how would it possibly steer without having somebody possessing the shoulders of the Incredible Hulk riding it? On a normal motorbike there is probably only two to

[1] Batman rides the Batpod in **The Dark Knight**. Its unusual design spurred Corbould to ask Christopher Nolan and production designer Nathan Crowley if they had ever ridden a motorbike. "They both replied 'no,'" reports Corbould, "and I attribute this fact to the reason that the Batpod was so unorthodox."

[1]

[2] The Batmobile races through the streets of Gotham City. The initial design did not include mudguards, which presented the problem of mud and stones being thrown up on the windscreen from the wide front wheels. "We thought that we would covertly hide some brushes behind the wheels to try and limit some of this debris," he says, "but just before filming commenced, Chris Nolan came over to me and said jokingly, 'Don't think I haven't seen the brushes behind the wheels, but tonight I will let you off.'

three square inches of rubber in contact with the ground, but here we were faced with a strip of rubber measuring 20 inches by four inches."

"Chris wanted the Batpod to look as little as a motorbike as possible and even refused to refer to it as a motorbike," adds Corbould. "After consulting with my crew I decided to quickly assemble a working prototype to see if it was remotely possible to ride and steer. After several amusing test runs we felt that there were possibilities for the Batpod to actually perform and set about designing and fabricating six vehicles."

The team used a 450cc single-cylinder engine concealed under the Batpod bodywork. French stunt rider Jean Pierre Goy was engaged to ride the vehicle and work on handling. "One of the biggest improvements he helped implement," says Corbould, "was to grind rubber off the outer limits of the front tires to form more of a radius rather than a long flat strip and if you study Jean Pierre in the film you will notice that he is

constantly shifting from one radius to the other rather than riding bolt upright."

One final consideration was Batman's flowing cape as he rides the Batpod. "Chris Nolan, as usual, had omitted to include mudguards over the wheels," says Corbould, "and I had great concerns that Batman's cape would get wrapped up in these and potentially pull him off. We assembled Jean Pierre and the costume and fitted several weak links that would break free should it get tangled with the wheel. Surprisingly, when Jean Pierre pulled away, the wind lifted the cape and kept it well clear of the wheel giving it a totally iconic look. I had to report to Chris and admit that my concerns were unjustified to which I received his usual wry 'I thought it might work' smile."

Inception

Corbould again teamed up with director Christopher Nolan for *Inception* (2010). A signature special effect in the film involved a rotating hotel corridor in which a "zero-gravity" fight between Arthur (Joseph Gordon-Levitt) and a number of henchmen would take place, while Arthur's friends are in various other character's subconscious states. "Chris spoke with me about the possibility of a revolving room," recalls Corbould, "and I mentioned that I had made a couple before, but then he asked me the question, 'How big can you make them?'"

The concepts for the corridor ultimately required a 120-foot build. To enable the corridor to rotate, Corbould's team fabricated six large, 30-foot diameter rings that were linked together with steelwork to form a large tombola-style tube. "This tube was then supported in a giant cradle with each ring resting on a set of drive wheels," explains Corbould. "These wheels were all linked by drive shafts and connected to two huge electric motors that worked in tandem via computer software. It was vital for us to have control of the motors by computer so we could accurately set ramp up/down speeds as well as maintaining the optimum speeds for the fight sequence to take place. It also gave us the means to perform emergency stops safely without risking damage to the mechanisms."

Engineer Paul Knowles oversaw steelwork fabrication in a large hangar at Cardington in Bedfordshire, UK. Says Corbould: "The giant steel rings were rolled from steel I-beam in three sections and then welded together in a jig to ensure that they were perfectly round. One by one the rings were lifted up and lowered into the giant cradle, before being connected by steel tubes. Once complete, the steel skeleton was powered up on the electric motors to test the rotating mechanism. When we were satisfied with its performance we handed it over to the construction department to build the set into."

Capturing the action inside the corridor was made possible by a camera built into the set that could track up and down its length as the corridor rotated. "Underneath the floor," says Corbould, "we attached a custom-built track attached to a camera mount going through a slot in the floor capable of working upside down and on its side whilst whizzing up and down the length of the set."

Gordon-Levitt rehearsed the fight scene in the revolving corridor for weeks with the stunt team. "We had designed the set to rotate at a maximum of six revolutions per minute," states Corbould, "but once rehearsing, we found that three revolutions was the optimum speed. There was a distinct change in actor performance above three revolutions—it changed from acting out a fight scene to suddenly fighting to stay on one's feet."

Corbould is particularly fond of the combination on *Inception* of both special and digital effects in the corridor sequence. "The CGI effects team, headed by Paul Franklin, played a massive part in the success of the corridors and zero-gravity scenes, as well as doing some showcase visual effects of their own, but I really felt we worked together as a perfect team on *Inception*."

[1] Arthur (Joseph Gordon-Levitt) fights an adversary inside the revolving corridor. One consideration Corbould had to contend with inside the corridor was how the lights would be powered in a moving set. "It was not feasible to have electric cables wrapping around it," he says, "so a large electrical slip ring was fabricated that bolted on one end and allowed electricity to be supplied to the set via a series of brass rings and spring-loaded contacts."

Skyfall

On Sam Mendes' *Skyfall* (2012), Corbould took film chases to yet another new level, this time when Bond (Daniel Craig) employs a train-mounted digger to rip the back off another train carriage as he pursues the mercenary Patrice (Ola Rapace).

Corbould's team decided to computerize all the movements of the digger for safety reasons. "This machine weighed in excess of 23 tons and it would have been catastrophic had it slid off the carriage," he says. "We also felt that it was imperative for the digger to only perform planned movements and not do anything unpredictable. We were able to program a complete move whilst stationary for crew and camera rehearsals and only when totally confident would we film the sequence at speed along the tracks."

Bond firstly knocks off a number of Volkswagen Beetle cars on the train carriage with the digger before running over more cars. "The most complex part of the scene was where the digger drove up the remaining Volkswagens and then extended its arm to rip the roof from the carriage in front," notes Corbould. "We specially prepared a lightweight section of carriage roof that the bucket dug into, and then inserted a small ten foot carriage between the digger and roof for it to fall onto."

As if the digger effect was not spectacular enough, Corbould was also called upon to stage the dramatic shot of a London underground train crashing through a tunnel roof. "The carriages of the train were 60-feet long and we really needed two of them to make the shot work, making a total of 120 feet," notes Corbould. "On investigation, real train carriages weighed 20 tons each, so we decided to make our own, but they still weighed in at five tons each. Then we needed space to get the train up to speed and then space to slow it down

[1] A shot leading up to the train and digger sequence.

[1]

[2] Patrice (Ola Rapace) shoots at Bond inside the digger atop the train carriage. "We ensured it stayed on the carriage by fabricating a super strong steel guide track along the center line of the flat back railway carriage," says Corbould, "and then fitting a massive captive skate that ran along this guide track."

once it crashed into the set. The result was a track stretching the entire length of the biggest stage in Europe—the 007 stage. Jason Leinster designed an overhead monorail track that supported the train on its approach and then allowed it to drop into the set and crash along the floor."

"The track was supported on huge steel goalposts spanning the set, installed by Dan Homewood and his engineering team," adds Corbould. "The floor was built up using lightweight materials by the construction department, so that when the train hit the floor it appeared to plow through solid brickwork. Sections of archway and ceiling were prepared for the train to collide with on its path across the set.

Movement of the train was achieved using a complex cable and pulley system connected to a truck outside the stage, which released from the cable once it started its descent. An incremental brake system helped stop the train, although a "good old trusty 30-ton wall of sandbags" was needed to bring it to a full halt.

"Ten cameras were placed around the set and after action was cued the train started its journey," says Corbould. "It crashed through the ceiling, plowed across the floor, and finally came to rest in the perfect position. Few people will have spotted that the train driver who was composited into the driver's cab was actually me—you would have to scan forward in slow motion to notice!"

3 > **Richard Edlund**

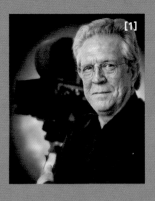

Few visual-effects supervisors carry the broad skills and experience held by Richard Edlund. A winner of four visual effects Oscars and three Academy Scientific and Engineering Awards, Edlund's career in the industry has also transcended the dramatic shift from photochemical, physical, and practical effects to the digital realm.

Edlund worked on each of the original *Star Wars* films, becoming a major force at Industrial Light & Magic where he helped pioneer the use of miniatures, motion control, and optical printers in visual effects. He won Oscars for all three movies and also for his visual effects supervision on *Raiders of the Lost Ark*, as well as scoring a nomination for *Poltergeist*. In 1983, Edlund formed his own effects company, Boss Film, and here contributed groundbreaking effects to films such as *Ghostbusters*, *2010*, *Die Hard*, *Poltergeist II: The Other Side*, *Cliffhanger*, *Alien³*, *Species*, *Multiplicity*, and *Air Force One*—in the process garnering another five Oscar nominations. Other visual effects film credits include *Bedazzled*, *The Stepford Wives*, *Charlie Wilson's War*, and *21 Jump Street*.

Edlund says he noticed the first real major shift to digital effects when Boss Film's commercial division began using Quantel's "Harry" video-compositing system in the mid-1980s. "You could go into a Harry session with a sow's ear and come out with a silk purse," comments Edlund. "It was so facile and there were so many possibilities in the digital world. Then I would have to come back and wrestle with the optical printer, and I would consider that to be sumo wrestling. You get thrown out of the ring several times!"

Edlund would take advantage of this digital technology, and its ability to provide fast shot turnarounds, when he was asked to produce effects on the final ascending-to-heaven sequence in *Ghost* (1990) for the purposes of a test screening. "What they had cut into the movie at that time was Patrick Swayze kissing Demi Moore and then walking up a mylar platform toward a bluescreen with grips in the shot! You couldn't have that scene at the end of the movie and expect the audience to be into it—it had to be ethereal and ghostly and powerful."

"I got a piece of workprint," recalls Edlund, "and went into a bay at the Post Group with Steve Price, who was a really great compositor. I brought some elements that had been shot on the Oxberry animation stand with an endoscope of Christmas tinsel and stuff like that. We brought these elements into the Harry and we put Patrick Swayze into this heaven environment, and were able to increase the resolution to make it work for film even though it was video."

All this had to be completed in two weeks, which was unheard of at that time in the film world. "On Monday I got the gig," says Edlund, "then Tuesday I went in and worked with Steve, and I think half a day on Wednesday. We then took the material and the guys did the up-res'ing on a film recorder. It came out great and on Friday I took the shot back over and they were dumbfounded! We did the whole sequence and—remember this was just on a workprint—we showed it to the studio and they all thought it was a final! So the movie tested extremely well and was an extreme hit."

"That's what really convinced me we were on the verge of greatness in the digital world," adds Edlund. "The difference between the photochemical world and the digital world is a complete gulf in ingenuity. A different kind of ingenuity is required to do a digital movie than a photochemical movie. The photochemical process is an unwilling adversarial process—you can trick it, but it's really difficult. For all effects though, you've really got to understand photography and treat it like a science and an art."

[1] Richard Edlund.

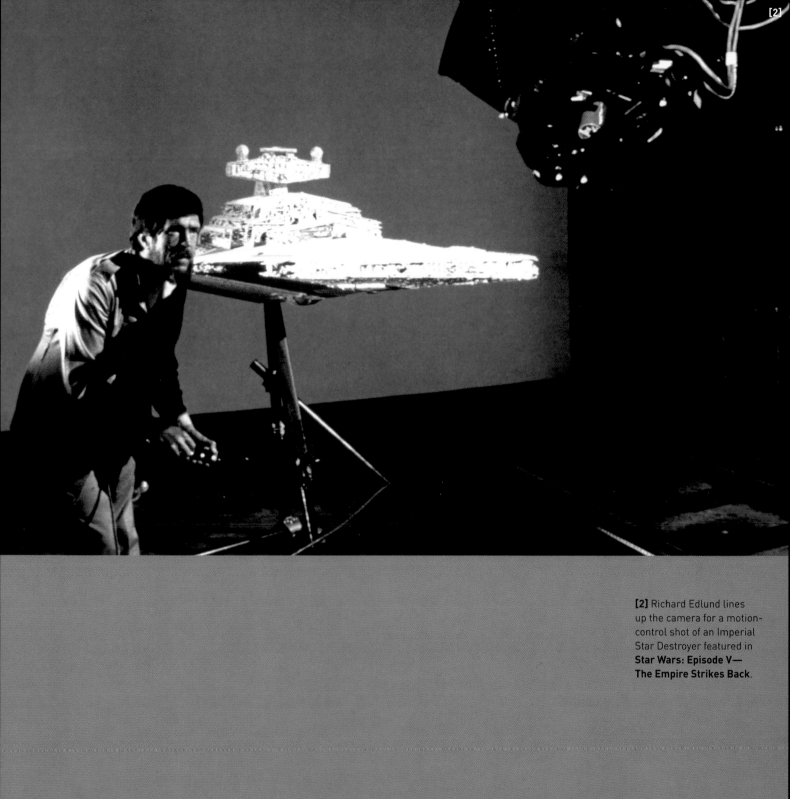

[2] Richard Edlund lines up the camera for a motion-control shot of an Imperial Star Destroyer featured in **Star Wars: Episode V— The Empire Strikes Back**.

Star Wars: Episode IV—A New Hope

Of all the signature images from George Lucas' *Star Wars: Episode IV—A New Hope* (1977)—and there are many—the opening shot of the Rebel Blockade Runner ship being pursued by an Imperial Star Destroyer is perhaps one of the most favored. "Everybody remembers that shot," says Edlund, who played a key part in designing and filming the final effect, which literally feels as if it is going over the audience's head.

The opening shot begins with a pan down from the titles crawl to reveal the Blockade Runner being fired on by the much, much larger spacecraft occupying almost the entire screen. The shot would spend a great deal of time in gestation while the technology needed to realize it was being developed. "We just kept talking about it and talking about it," says Edlund. "Initially, George was thinking we'd build a big model and truck the camera over it. But we didn't have enough track to do that. We were getting toward the end of production and we didn't have that opening shot and I just started to get worried about it."

Other spaceships and shots in the film were being realized at Industrial Light & Magic with intricately detailed models and an innovative computer-controlled motion-control camera system. Here, a spaceship model

[1] The Millennium Falcon model is suspended on a rig to be filmed with motion control. A 12-channel motion-control system was used that controlled a camera track, pan, tilt, roll, and any movement of the model itself.

[2] The Millennium Falcon, positioned on a blue pylon that would be matted out during the optical compositing stage.

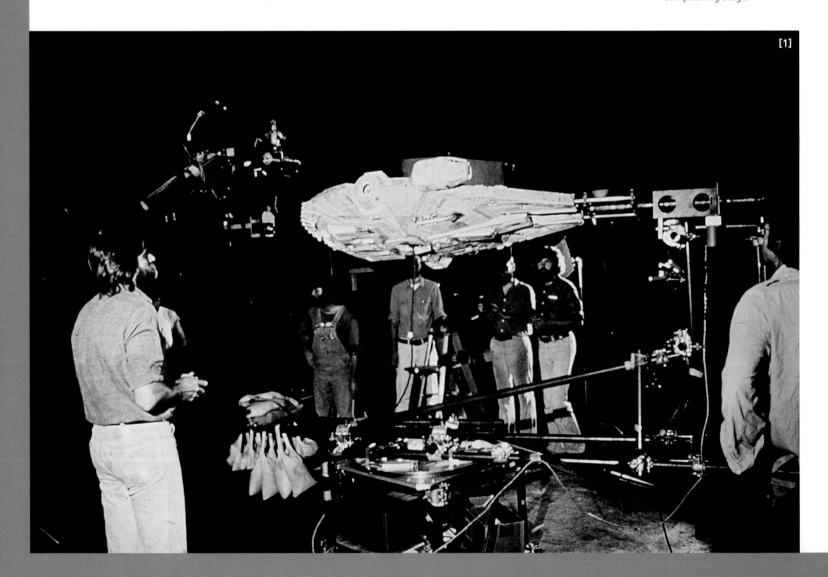

[1]

would be filmed against bluescreen in a stationary position, while the camera moved around it. When that footage was composited against a star field or another object or environment, it provided the illusion of movement.

To finally nail the film's opening shot, Edlund decided to prepare a test. "We had a Star Destroyer model and it was finished very well on the bottom and on one side. I asked model maker Grant McCune to trick out the bottom of the model as best as possible and especially asked for fine detail work on the docking bay on the bottom. And then I asked him to make a Rebel Blockade Runner that was four inches long."

"I stuck the tiny Blockade Runner model on the underside of the Star Destroyer with a paper clip that was straightened out," continues Edlund. "Then we had this 24mm lens that would go incredibly close to these models. I could tilt the lens and hold horizontal focus very well. I could basically scrape the surface of the model with the lens—the lens actually touched the surface of the model at a couple of points during the shot. So I figured out a length of the shot and did a test and we were dumbfounded the next day—it was just amazing how well it worked. My thinking was that this is probably the most important shot of the movie—if we don't grab the audience with the beginning shot of the movie we're in trouble."

Edlund has fond memories, too, of working with the Millennium Falcon model. "The Falcon was this much bigger ship—it weighed over one hundred pounds and required a two-and-a-half inch pylon to hold it up. So it was much more difficult to shoot, but we got some incredible shots out of it."

"It's funny, thinking back," he says. "As effects guys we had all been experimenting in this area and then suddenly we were like the Black Hawks—there was no one around like us and we were able to put 365 shots together for the movie."

Raiders of the Lost Ark

On Steven Spielberg's *Raiders of the Lost Ark* (1981), Edlund was charged with depicting the surge of God rays and catastrophic energy bolts that kill a group of Nazi soldiers after they open the Ark of the Covenant. Edlund knew that each individual soldier had to suffer the fate of lightning ripping through their body. The actual lightning would be an animated effect completed by Industrial Light & Magic, but a major concern was acquiring the appropriate "contact lighting" on each actor as the energy bolts hit.

The solution essentially involved a personal lighting system and a method that provided a specific look to the lighting. "Firstly," explains Edlund, "I basically created a filter that had grooves carved into the glass in the shape of a fan—kind of like a Japanese fan opening up with grooves. The idea there was that if you put that in front of the lens, instead of having a straight across flare, the flare was arced, so you had a winged flare."

That flare was enhanced by a lighting rig worn by each actor playing a Nazi. "We had an asbestos pad and a little shoulder strap arrangement that would go over the neck of the actor," explains Edlund. "In the middle of this pad was a special flashbulb I had discovered had been developed in the middle of the 1950s for super high-speed cameras."

The bulb would flash, but not at a usual speed. "Instead of going off in 1/50 of a second, it would go in two seconds," says Edlund. "So it would build in intensity, be like sunlight for two seconds, and then it would trail off. And this was going to be inside the shirt of the Nazi. On each actor we scribed the shirt so that it would burn open and then each Nazi had in front of this rig a little spotlight on a gooseneck wire rig that would light his face."

This meant that the actors' faces were lit by the spotlight at the same time as the flash was triggered on the back. "Each guy had his own trigger," notes Edlund. "We told them don't flash right away, maybe half a second delay so they don't all go off at the exact same

[1] Ghoulish beings emerge from the Ark, partly realized with armatures filmed underwater to create an ethereal and classic cape-flowing look.

[1]

moment—make it random. Then we had to animate all the lightning that came out."

Interestingly, filming of the live action Ark opening scenes could only be partially completed on sets at Elstree Studios in London, due to time constraints. "So we decided we would shoot only the long shots," says Edlund. "Then I'd go through with production designer Norman Reynolds and pick backgrounds of the Styrofoam set and fill up a couple of vans full of set pieces, and we'd shoot close-ups back in Marin County."

Prior to the lightning effects, the opening of the Ark also triggers the release of flying ghosts. These were achieved by filming ghost armatures in a water tank—giving them a flowing feel—and then optically composting them with lighting effects in the scene. Live-action photography of an actress in skeletal makeup, optically matched with a practical skeleton piece, also made it into the sequence.

[2] One of the skeleton-like creations used to show the escape of souls from the opened Ark.

[3] The Nazis open the Ark of the Covenant, releasing a wave of dark souls and energy rays.

Ghostbusters

When Ivan Reitman's *Ghostbusters* hit cinema screens in 1984, few people imagined how massive the film would be—and that included Edlund himself as its visual effects supervisor. "We were making this film," he recalls, "with strange ghosts, a green slime ghost, a giant Marshmallow Man, and a bunch of *Saturday Night Live* comedians. So we'd see the rushes each day and just be laughing the whole time, not really knowing if audiences were going to love it too."

But they did, especially some of the film's big surprises, such as the appearance of the giant Stay Puft Marshmallow Man, conjured up as a new form for evil god Gozer. Shots of the 100-foot monster wreaking havoc in New York would be achieved using multiple techniques, ranging from an actor in a suit, to miniatures, live-action street footage, matte paintings, and optical compositing.

"How we first revealed the Marshmallow Man was an interesting story," says Edlund. "That was filmed on a matte camera. We had miniatures and then we did a pan across the rooftop of a building, and then we see a slot between the two buildings. And then we're tracking the camera right to left and we see this big white face. Then you see his sailor hat briefly and you cut to Dan Akroyd saying, 'What did you do, Ray?' I just remember that as one of the funniest lines in the film."

"There's another shot," describes Edlund, "where the Ghostbusters are on top of the temple and they're looking down and they see the Marshmallow Man walking down on Central Park West. That's basically on a miniature. It's a forced perspective miniature street with nine-inch long cars that were re-purposed from real toys, a miniature Central Park, even a miniature fire hydrant spurting out sand to look like water, and

[1] The Ghostbusters use their proton packs—effects for the energy beams were achieved with hand-drawn animation composited into live-action photography on an optical printer.

[1]

[2] The Stay Puft Marshmallow Man, one of **Ghostbusters**' most memorable characters. The existence of the fictional promotional character is hinted earlier in the film on a packet of marshmallows in one scene and in graffiti outside the Ghostbusters headquarters. Here the monster tramples over Columbus Circle—a shot consisting of a bluescreen plate of the Marshmallow Man performer, and live-action photography of the New York street scene.

then there's a matte painting on the left and the building on the right is a matte painting. The guys were shot against a bluescreen."

The forced-perspective set employed a technique that enabled the Marshmallow Man to appear much larger in frame than he really was. Into that forced-perspective miniature set was composited footage of Bill Bryan in a marshmallow suit. Bryan also worked as a sculptor on the actual design and then fabrication of the final suit, made of fine-celled Scott foam sitting over the top of suitably shaped body-pods along with a cable-operated head piece. Since the Marshmallow Man would be shown burning as the Ghostbusters attack with their proton backs, the suit incorporated insulating Pyrothane and fire-resistant Nomex layers.

A later view sees the Marshmallow Man stomp onto Columbus Circle in New York City. "That was a bluescreen Marshmallow Man and we shot Bill at 60- or 72-frames per second just to give the right weight. For the background plate we had all these New York extras. We only got one take because we did it with a whole bunch of taxi cabs in the foreground. And it was real cold—we were in November—I only had a short jacket on and I wish I didn't!"

Multiplicity

In 1996, Edlund re-teamed with *Ghostbusters* actor, Harold Ramis, when Ramis directed *Multiplicity*, the story of construction worker Doug Kinney (Michael Keaton) who clones himself, causing personal mayhem in the process.

With shots entailing up to four Michael Keatons in the frame at one time, visual effects were always going to be necessary. Edlund proposed a complex, but foolproof system involving a silent, motion-control setup, camera-head encoder, and on-set split-screen feedback from a nearby trailer for getting the clone shots done. Firstly, the scenes would be shot with Keaton and up to three stand-ins playing the clones. The first take was the key shot, as every take that followed had to match the camera movement and action.

To ensure that actor movement could be replicated, Edlund devised a camera head with a gun-like laser sight. "An operator would follow the footsteps of, say, the stand-in who was the second guy that Michael was playing," explains Edlund. "The laser sight was in sync with a video camera that the stand-in was carrying at head height. This meant that Michael could play to his second character, and his second character would then see what the stand-in was shooting, which was the first Michael. So the eyeline was perfect. Basically, Michael was looking at a camera that was where his head was going to be in the next shot."

Keaton would then change into the wardrobe and makeup for the next take to play another version of himself. The down time meant that Edlund's crew in the trailer could quickly establish traveling split screens and composites, with the process continuing up to four times for the four different Keaton roles. Occasionally, takes would be shot with small pieces of bluescreen

[1] In this scene, the clones are seated on a couch while the real Doug stands behind them. Edlund notes that some digital intervention took place to fix a few cushions and overlaps necessary for such complicated shots. To shoot multiple Keatons in the scene, Edlund adapted a silent, motion-control camera system, including a dolly and a boom that had originally been built for **Alien³**.

[2] With Michael Keaton playing multiple roles and requiring a change in clothing, hair, and makeup between takes, the film shoot reached a staggering 99 days.

or greenscreen in place where the actor might walk past, facilitating an easier composite.

Edlund says the process worked surprisingly well and resulted in some stand-out shots. "There was one scene where Michael's character hands himself a plate with a sandwich on it," recalls the visual effects supervisor. "The way we did that was in take one, Michael would act with his downstage arm behind his back. The second take we'd do with the stand-in who would be in the shot and he would hand the plate to Michael, but his hand was going to be replaced as Michael's hand. So we basically rotoscoped Michael's arm at his shoulder and used the stand-in's hand. It lined up perfectly so we used that trick a number of times."

A beer can toss between the clones was another signature shot. "Michael is sitting on the couch and talking to his clone, filmed with his stand-in, and throws him a beer," outlines Edlund. "In our second take, the stand-in had to throw Michael the beer and then Michael caught it. We checked the line up in our trailer and it absolutely worked perfectly! We didn't need to do any rotoscoping clean up at all."

"I've often said," notes Edlund, "that if I finish a show and I feel it's perfect, I'm ready to retire. Well *Multiplicity* really did go well, but I didn't retire! It's one of my very favorites, and one of my favorite directors to have worked with in Harold Ramis."

4 > Scott Farrar

In the visual effects world, Scott Farrar is synonymous with the memorable robotic CG characters of the *Transformers* films. But the senior visual effects supervisor, who joined Industrial Light & Magic in 1981, began his career in the days of motion-control camera and optical compositing. Farrar has fond memories of these days working in the practical side of effects filmmaking. "We were working with hand-made machines that had electric motors," he says, "trying to print pictures with mattes with unbelievable accuracy considering the mechanics that are required to do that. It's staggering."

Farrar won an Academy Award for achievement in visual effects for *Cocoon* (1985). He says the experience crafting the miniature spaceship and light-emitting alien effects for the Ron Howard film is typical of his work at ILM: "It involved getting artwork and then figuring out how to basically 'make' the artwork. It's a crazy, crazy world we live in—they trust us that somehow at the end of the day we'll hand in some pretty cool images. And we do!"

Farrar has been nominated for a visual effects Oscar a further five times (for *Backdraft*, *AI: Artificial Intelligence*, *The Chronicles of Narnia: The Lion, the Witch and the Wardrobe*, *Transformers*, and *Transformers: Dark of the Moon*). His other film credits include such visual effects milestones as *Star Trek: The Motion Picture*, *Star Trek II: The Wrath of Khan*, *Star Wars: Episode VI—The Return of the Jedi*, the *Back to the Future* trilogy, *Star Trek VI: The Undiscovered Country*, *Jurassic Park*, *Casper*, *Congo*, *Deep Impact*, *Star Wars: Episode I—The Phantom Menace*, *Minority Report*, *Peter Pan*, *Transformers: Revenge of the Fallen*, *Transformers: Age of Extinction*, and *World War Z*. A rewarding aspect of contributing to so many films, says Farrar, is the ability to learn something new on each film and pass on that knowledge to the next effect or character he works on.

"On *Backdraft*, for example, Ron Howard thought that part of the puzzle should be that the fire is sort of a beast—a character. We got lots of prep time to test fire shots on this burn stage in Chicago, which is where we came up with the upside-down fire—the fire on the ceiling—and starving it of oxygen and getting these fantasy swirls and spinners that we could never get from a practical fire on the floor."

"And with *Casper*," continues Farrar, "I got so heavily engrossed in (the painter) Johannes Vermeer. We were trying to come up with new ways of lighting, especially computer graphics. This was one of the first films with a CG-animated character all the way through, and it was very hard then to do, especially with a character you see through. I was studying Vermeer and how light and shadow plays on things. That's where you learn. How do you make things look real in a painting—a ceramic jug or a cloth that's made out of finely woven velvet, for example? How does a painter do that, and how do we do that in computer graphics? You learn from the masters."

Having traversed both the mechanical and digital worlds of visual effects, Farrar says his vast experience in the pre-digital age has been vital to his work now. "We created thousands of shots on motion-control cameras using stepper motors," notes Farrar. "You can graph out the path of motion of the recorded motor, and over time it's plus or minus, whether it's turning one direction or another—that's basically a spline curve. And everything in computer graphics and animation is a spline curve. I call it the 'dreaded spline!' It's so easy for it to be smooth, just like the perfection in the computer, which I call the 'devil incarnate.' The thing we're trying to do in visual effects is defeat the perfection created by the computer, because real life and the real world does not look perfect."

That's a philosophy Farrar has brought into some of the more heavy CG shows he's worked on such as the *Transformers* films. "I started in photography," says Farrar. "I think most people who are in the visual effects industry today come from computer graphics backgrounds, but a few of us come from art and

[1] Scott Farrar at the 8th Annual Visual Effects Society VES Awards in LA in 2010.

[2] Optimus Prime—voiced by Peter Cullen, who also voiced the original animated series—was made up of 10,108 CG parts.

photography, and I really think that's an important aspect because doing that photography means you're dealing with the real world all the time and trying to capture moments."

"You have to make split-second decisions when you're shooting," he adds. "You're always changing your plan because you're going to see something better—and that's exactly the thing that should impact a visual effects shot. There should be spontaneity to the look of a shot, and that's what I try and bring in a way to visual effects."

[2]

Back to the Future trilogy

Farrar worked on each of Robert Zemeckis' *Back to the Future* films under overall visual effects supervisor Ken Ralston at ILM. On the first movie, Farrar was an effects cameraman, moving to effects supervisor for the second and third parts of the time travel trilogy. The films would showcase a combination of live action, miniatures, and hand-animated effects for the time machine, while advanced split-screening allowed actors to play multiple roles; early CG painting tools were used to erase wires.

"*Back to the Future* was the combination of all of those things," notes Farrar, "but with a really strong artistic drive that for its time felt kind of real. There were really creative ideas from writer Bob Gale and Bob Zemeckis— they had such a great script." Farrar recalls the specific moment that he started on the trilogy. "Four of us were doing *Cocoon* at the time," he says. "I was shooting the spaceship and we got a call about 3 o'clock in the afternoon saying, 'Hey you guys, can you wrap up the shot you're shooting today with the miniature spaceship and get on a plane and get down here because we're shooting all night at the backlot at Universal?' There were many days like that where we'd work 24 hours a day, just because there were so few crews."

In *Back to the Future Part II*, Doc Brown (Christopher Lloyd) and Marty McFly (Michael J. Fox) travel to 2015 in a retrofitted-for-flight DeLorean. Shots featuring the flying car were achieved with a miniature motion-controlled model shot on bluescreen and integrated into miniature sets and matte-painted environments. The film also often cleverly transitioned from the model DeLorean to the live-action full-sized vehicle via an invisible wipe device.

The memorable hoverboard chase sequence from Part II, echoing a skateboard sequence in the first film, made early use of digital wire removal. Here, Marty is pursued around the Hill Valley town square, a set filmed

[1] Griff Tannen's (Thomas F. Wilson) gang pursues Marty McFly on their hoverboards in **Back to the Future Part II**.

[1]

The DeLorean time machine in **Back to the Future**—ILM would build a matching 1/5 miniature scale model of the vehicle for flying shots and stunt effects throughout the trilogy.

at Universal Studios. The actors were shot either being held by a strong truck-based rig or on overhead wires. Early wire-removal software written at ILM allowed artists to interpolate the image to the right and left of the practical wires holding the actors to make it appear as if they were hovering.

Further innovations in this second film included a specialized camera—dubbed the VistaGlide—devised by ILM that allowed for seamless split-screens. This meant the same actor could play different parts in the same shot, such as when Fox performed the roles of his older self, son, and daughter during the dinner scene. "This was basically a VistaVision camera," explains Farrar, "with a blimp on a Panther dolly that let you record a shot,

save that move, and then have your actor go away and come back in different clothing and be on the other side of the screen."

"We also had motion-control equipment that ran things when Michael J. Fox hands himself a plate of chicken," says Farrar. "We had motion-control drivers lifting the plate and moving it so he could just take it. We came up with all those gags—that was it in those days, we just made all this stuff up! That's what we did. People were giving us money to go and figure this stuff out."

Minority Report

When Steven Spielberg began researching how to make *Minority Report* (2002)—his science-fiction thriller set in 2054 A.D. in a world where "PreCrime" police officers apprehend criminals before they have committed an offence—the director and Farrar looked for ways to distinguish the film from other films depicting the future. Spielberg's approach was to consult a unique forum of scientists who gathered to consider the kinds of technologies that might exist in the mid-21st century. Out of that collaboration came such final film elements as a magnetic levitation—or "Maglev"—transportation system, interactive sliding screens, and new police equipment, such as "sick sticks" and jet packs.

It was Farrar's job to help translate these scientific predictions into realistic on-screen imagery. "The first challenge was how do you create a futuristic city with these Maglev cars," says Farrar. "Hollywood was always taking a chassis and putting a modern style car body on it, but in some films you see it bouncing around like a real car and it didn't look like it was floating. We had to make it look real."

Farrar suggested to Spielberg that the transportation system and any futuristic buildings should be integrated into the modern day cityscape of Washington D.C. and Virginia where scenes were set. "I went to Steven and told him I thought it'd be far more interesting if our roads and buildings were built on top of the existing city. That's really what happens today where old parts of a city are just added to. That meant that our Maglev roads were all twists and turns as they passed through old and new areas."

One of the most dramatic Maglev scenes features Tom Cruise's character, John Anderton—now accused of a future murder himself—exiting a vehicle and jumping from car to car as they pass over the side of a building. "That sequence was great for me," recalls Farrar. "It was one of the first times I got to direct a second unit. It was just Tom and myself, and my own mini-crew. We had a previs sequence mapping how we were going to do it and how Tom would jump from car to car. Gosh that was a lot of fun—I still remember that. It's sort of like film school. We'd just talk and come up with ideas to embellish what

[1] PreCrime officers arrive via jetpacks in the hope of arresting John Anderton (Tom Cruise). Visual effects artists would paint out wires holding the actors, as well as an elaborate gantry system that allowed them to fly. Heat haze and jet exhaust was also added.

[1]

[2] Anderton atop a Maglev vehicle. Scenes like this were generally filmed with Cruise performing on a bluescreen stage, on a practical car, which would later be incorporated into digital backgrounds by ILM, under Farrar's supervision.

we were doing. It was fun! What's really great about filmmaking is that it becomes very personal and you're just coming up with ideas beyond what is scripted or beyond the previs. If you have a cool idea, if it's really great, it's going to end up in the movie."

Farrar also supervised visual effects for a sequence in which Anderton continues to evade his fellow police pursuers sporting jet packs in an alleyway. The scene was largely filmed practically on the Warner Bros. backlot, with actors and stunt performers rigged on a gantry fitted with infinity loop line with a cable system, and motors and controllers that could make a person fly while they also ascended or descended.

"We were getting much better at that time in painting out wires," explains Farrar, "so I said I don't care how thick the wire is—make sure everybody's safe. We were ready to take over with a CG version of the

performers, but we didn't need to because everything looked so good. I'd get asked, 'Do you feel okay about Tom Cruise doing some potentially dangerous wire work?' but I was really confident in Tom, who loved doing all his own stunts."

Transformers

Farrar has been the visual effects supervisor on each film in director Michael Bay's wildly successful *Transformers* franchise, which started in 2007. But crafting realistic live-action versions of the famous Hasbro robots was not, at least initially, plain sailing. "A lot of the initial designs for the Transformers were very alien in style," relates Farrar. "We started doing these designs and building them at ILM and it was a disaster—they didn't look good at all! It was all very CG and as a viewer you really didn't know what the robots were meant to be made of."

The solution—determined by both Bay and Farrar—was to go back to the roots of the characters. "We thought, well, they're supposed to be cars, so we started adding in pieces of cars such as a muffler, or a rotor, or a shock absorber, as well as pistons and gears, and we decided to make them very obviously made of car parts," says Farrar. "We got about 6,000 photos of these car parts and started putting all these parts onto the robots. And suddenly it started looking real."

But that was only the first step. The robots also had to be infused with realistic lighting, reflectance, and color that was true to their metallic car parts and surfaces. "We wanted to make these things look so real that you'd be watching the movie and be convinced that it was a real metal puppet."

Luckily, several artists at ILM had previously worked in the studio's model shop and were familiar with fabricating materials. "We knew that one problem with the computer was that it likes to make everything straight and perfectly flat," says Farrar. "But that didn't work for our creatures. They needed to have compound curves that would emulate automotive body shapes—we had to do that because the reflectance angle of the sun for the glints has to roll over those curves. Michael Bay and I were keenly aware of making the sheen and the lighting look real, but you couldn't do it without the proper shape."

The result was that each part had to be broken down into various layers, just like a car panel might have a metal flake paint with a clear-coat finish on top.

[1]

[1] The Autobot Bumblebee transforms into a 1974 Chevrolet Camero and a 2007 version in the film. His bipedal form is made up of 7608 polygons, 1,511,727 rig nodes, and 19,722 texture maps.

[2] The Decepticon Bonecrusher engages Optimus Prime on a freeway. Effects artists referenced martial arts fighting footage and motion capture to bring some of the robot fight scenes to life.

"It's got to be broken down so all the interpolation in the computer reads it," explains Farrar. "It was something like four to 16 layers of information for a single part so that it would read correctly when seen in the film."

A new approach was also required to solve the complex animations as the robots transformed from bipedal form to vehicles and vice versa. Ultimately, effects artists and technicians at ILM would develop specific tools to help them with these transformations, which they advanced on each *Transformers* film.

"Again," says Farrar, "this was a long combination of failures and successes. Doing the transformations still required somebody—usually a single animator—to plan the paths of each piece. For instance, parts might spiral out of the chest and fly down and around then disappear behind the body and, at the same time, morph into different sizes and shapes. It's a painstaking process doing these cutting-edge visual effects and no matter what you've done it's a little bit different every time—it seems like every single movie is a prototype."

Transformers sequels

On each subsequent *Transformers* film—*Return of the Fallen*, *Dark of the Moon*, and *Age of Extinction*—Farrar upped the ante on the number of characters that would be featured on screen, the complexity of transformations and the scale of destruction. Major challenges on these *Transformers* sequels ranged from one of ILM's most complicated CG assets—the Decepticon Destroyer, which required 52,632 parts made from nearly 12 million polygons—to the large-scale destruction of Chicago skyscrapers in *Dark of the Moon*, and the rampaging Dinobots in *Age of Extinction*.

ILM's digital model for Optimus Prime in *Age of Extinction* had also come a long way from its beginnings, and was now made up of 2.7 million vertices and 6,732

pieces. All the while, Farrar sought to maintain a level of authenticity for the character. "There's the initial transformation of Optimus in Monument Valley in this latest film," highlights Farrar. "We do a spiral dolly around him and initially I had some big problems because there were some pieces that weren't turning toward the light as I wanted them to. You need to move certain pieces faster than others—it's showmanship— you're trying to make a cool shot in spite of everything else. That shot was finally finished less than a month before the movie was delivered."

Age of Extinction would be the first time audiences witnessed the film appearance of the Dinobots—beloved from the animated series. For Farrar, it was a blast to

[1] Director Michael Bay demonstrates to actress Nicola Peltz on the set of **Age of Extinction** how a Decepticon will attack, using a stand-in prop that will later be replaced by ILM.

[1]

[2] The Dinobot leader Grimlock. Background plates for this shot were filmed at the Wolong National Nature Reserve in China, with ILM creating the fire-breathing digital creature.

include them. "Wasn't that fun!" he exclaims. "Our company did *Jurassic Park*, of course, so it was a lot of fun taking the idea of a dinosaur that usually has skin and bones and muscle, and turning it into a mechanical version. Initially it was a little challenging, because the art provided to us didn't show pistons or joints or bearings where the jaw might be mounted to the skull. So we started building these things and adding mechanical pieces with nuts and bolts, and they started looking more like a machine."

Farrar was drawn early to the idea that Optimus would be riding the Dinobot leader, Grimlock, into battle. "That was straight from a John Ford western where you have the close-up of John Wayne riding on his faithful stead with the head of the horse in the foreground and the rider in the background," says Farrar. "I just loved that idea."

As they had done with the vehicle Transformers, ILM weathered the Dinobots for a more realistic appearance. "The patina and how mossy or copper-affected or aged the Dinobots looked was important," notes Farrar. "You want something interesting, but it's got to read like a real thing. If it's an aged model you want it to look properly aged."

"In fact," adds Farrar, "for this whole movie my approach in simple terms was to be a lot dirtier. We didn't feature the characters with perfect lighting anymore—it was rougher and darker, and we even put them in shadow. With the Dinobots we wanted them to feel like machines that were spitting and spluttering, and they always have gas emitting from somewhere—just to keep it messy all of the time, even to the point where they're splattering the lens with liquid."

World War Z

Solving on-set challenges is something Farrar has been called upon to do on numerous films. With Marc Forster's zombie outbreak film, *World War Z* (2013), the visual effects supervisor was faced with a more unusual problem—he came on board after the film had been shot, with the filmmakers looking to refine the edit and re-shoot the ending.

Farrar's first consideration was to review the visual effects already underway, starting with the designs for the zombies and their behaviors. "I saw all this artwork that had been done, but wasn't in the movie," he says, "and I thought it was fabulous. They'd even done some test shots. I thought, 'Wow these ideas are thoroughly

exciting, we've got to get them in the movie! If you haven't done these shots already we've got to do these shots and get some of these things happening.'"

"So I tried to steer things toward exciting ideas they'd already created," adds Farrar. "With that, they started to re-evaluate what the movie was, adding more shots of the ant-like behavior of the zombies, so the audience understood what the cause of this behavior was."

Farrar says he approached the creation of the film's zombie walk cycles, their attack techniques, and the way they group together using human pyramids as if it was "pseudo-science." "What if it was real?" he asked the visual effects crew. "We would spend hours talking about

[1] The zombies form a wave of bodies in an attempt to scale a protective wall in Israel, in this shot completed by MPC. The studio crafted 3,000 different wardrobe outfits and utilized their proprietary crowd tool and rigid body dynamic solver for the swarming shots.

[1]

[2] Scenes of zombies
launching themselves from
a rooftop in New Jersey made
use of actors filmed against
greenscreen, with Cinesite
performing digital take-overs
as they go over the edge.

the behavior and how the zombies would act. So once
bitten, the former humans reacted as if a virus takes
over—they can't control themselves and they don't even
think about their own personal safety anymore. And now
they're willing to launch themselves off a building onto
concrete and lead with the head and not even put their
arms out in front to save themselves. The Zs only live
for the bite."

The final shots in the film made use of highly detailed
digital zombies, as well as swarms created with CG
crowd systems for epic scenes. However, the film's
final act became a decidedly more personal experience
than had originally been filmed. "I thought what was
finally created with the second and third acts was really

intense," states Farrar. "You didn't quite know what was
going on in the beginning, then you start to understand
it a little bit more in the middle, but then it becomes a
very personal story—that's what was missing. Brad Pitt's
character never really had his own confrontation—one
on one—with a zombie. The story needed that personal
moment. That's ultimately why the film really worked in
the end, when he confronted the single zombie."

5 > Paul Franklin

Paul Franklin has supervised visual effects in films about superheroes, wizards, and people who enter the minds of others. His credits include _Pitch Black_, _Batman Begins_, _The Dark Knight_, _The Dark Knight Rises_, _Harry Potter and the Order of the Phoenix_, _Harry Potter and the Half-Blood Prince_, _Inception_, and _Interstellar_, winning an Academy Award for achievement in visual effects for both of those latter films.

[1] Paul Franklin.

Although he may have worked on some major Hollywood blockbusters, Franklin's educational background was in sculpture. "I did large metal work and stone carving," he says, "very much in the world of abstract fine art. However, running alongside my university course I was doing more commercial kinds of art—student theater design, magazine design, and one of the things I got into was making short films in the late 1980s. I was recording the sound, making props, even engaging bad acting! I also got into the editing, which included the title graphics for these short films."

At the time, Franklin worked for a small corporate video company. "They had a Commodore Amiga computer and I'd always been fascinated by the idea of 3D computer graphics. Pixar and ILM had been doing amazing things, but in terms of regular people, the Amiga was an introduction for a lot of us. So I began making little animated sequences on this computer. That actually meant I built up a skill base that allowed me to get a job as a computer animator working for a British gaming company called Psygnosis."

It was here that Franklin had access to "Hollywood standard" hardware. "They had bought Silicon Graphics workstations to run Softimage (animation software) back in 1991," he recalls. "The guys were quite happy for me to use the machines in downtime after work. So I was still working with my friends on short films and I became the in-house visual effects guy, making animated scenes for these short films."

Eventually Franklin turned his eye to the growing visual effects community in London (which was still small then by Hollywood standards), moving to The Moving Picture Company as an animator to work on television commercials, idents, and some feature films.

In 1998, he left with several colleagues to form Double Negative and create visual effects for _Pitch Black_. Many films followed, but it would be Double Negative's association with both the _Harry Potter_ franchise and the _Batman_ films that would propel the studio onto the international stage.

In _The Order of the Phoenix_, for example, Double Negative would employ a fully digital set for the first time in a _Harry Potter_ film for the Hall of Prophecies. Here, the characters encountered rows of crystal spheres on glass shelves, an effect that required clever techniques in ray tracing and compositing, especially when the spheres are blown apart.

For _Interstellar_, Franklin oversaw a complicated collection of practical effects, miniatures, and digital imagery for the Christopher Nolan film. In particular, CG renders of wormholes and black holes were carried out to represent the most recent scientific research on what these phenomena would actually look like. Some of those renders were even projected on-set during filming through spacecraft windows, helping to provide the actors and filmmakers with a sense of the final galactic imagery.

Double Negative is now one of the biggest effects houses in the world, but according to Franklin, its early days were a struggle. "I often say to people that if we'd known how difficult it would be to get a company up and running in those first five years, we probably wouldn't have bothered. There were times when I didn't know how we were going to get through it—the demands of the work, getting staff, keeping an even keel. Getting the company into a robust shape to weather the cyclical demands of the film industry was a challenge," adds Franklin.

[2] Astronauts explore an icy planet in the hope it might be a new home for Earth's remaining inhabitants, in **Interstellar**. Locations in Iceland were augmented by Double Negative to form the final shot.

Pitch Black

David Twohy's *Pitch Black* (2000) would serve as a proving ground for Franklin and his colleagues at their newly-established visual effects facility, Double Negative. The science-fiction film introduced prisoner Richard B. Riddick (Vin Diesel), whose spacecraft crash lands on a desert planet inhabited by predatory creatures. Double Negative largely handled CG versions of the creatures, with Franklin responsible for setting up the studio's 3D department while production on the film had already begun.

"We started Double Negative and on day one it was pretty much just me and my cell phone in Soho, London, trying to hire people and find out where our hardware had gotten to—it was tied up in a warehouse somewhere," recalls Franklin. "Some of the guys had already shipped out to Australia and were shooting the movie in Coober Pedy—I subsequently went out to join them on the Gold Coast where the sound stages were."

"We were focused on 'Dneg' getting up and running, getting our team up and running, and trying to prove ourselves," adds Franklin. "It was a little bit seat of the pants, adding people and machines to the show, but for a long time there were only four or five of us working on it. It was quite a challenge setting up the 3D department in Australia, as my tech support was 10,000 miles away in London. So it was quite stressful doing it all. We were working days in the studio making animations and tests, and trying to rig the creatures in Maya 1.0, pretty much the first version of the popular 3D software. The software was incredibly capable and powerful, but somewhat unreliable back then."

Double Negative based its CG creatures—dubbed "bio-raptors"—on practical versions designed by Patrick Tatopolous and built by John Cox's Creature Workshop. "We had these full-sized sculpts of the creatures that we then scanned as the basis for our CG models,"

[1] The bio-raptors are revealed in this fiery **Pitch Black** shot. Double Negative used practical animatronic puppets created by John Cox's Creature Workshop as the basis for creating their digital counterparts.

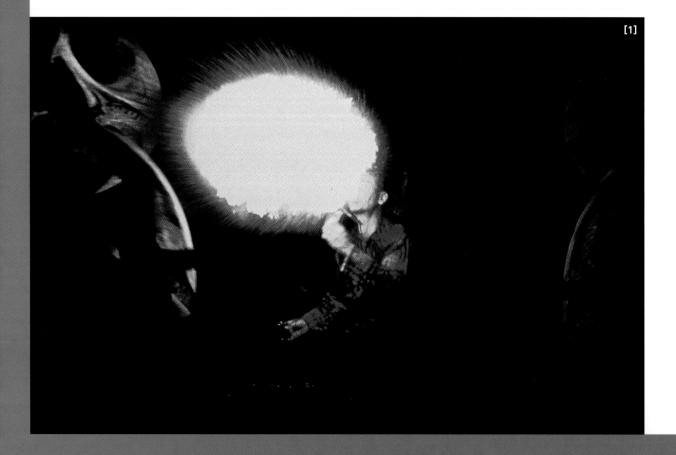

[1]

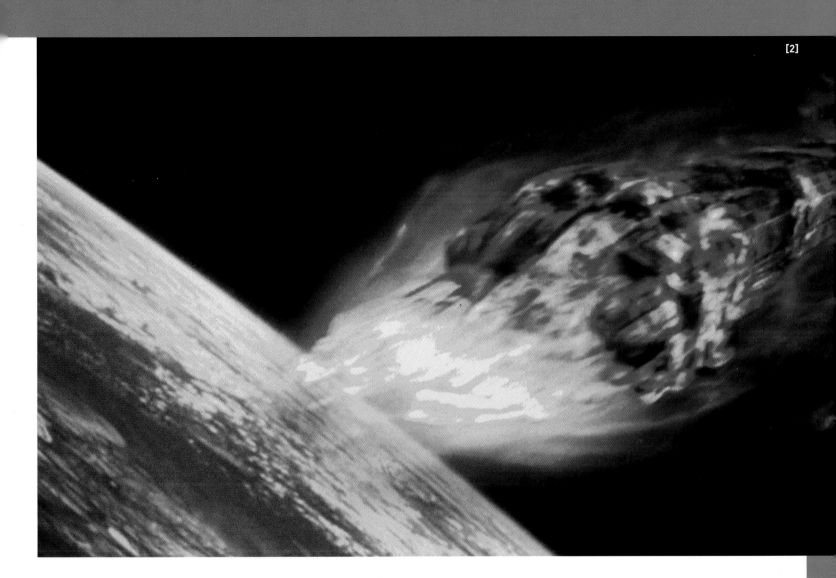

[2] A scene from the opening of the film as a freighter crash lands on the planet.

says Franklin. "The original intention was to have a lot more animatronics in the film, but because of budget constraints the physical effects were limited to hand shots or close-ups of the creatures. Still, there was a lot of practical in-camera special effects work—that rainstorm that happens at the end of the film was shot almost entirely at the Gold Coast studios."

"The scope of our digital work did expand where the animatronics left off," notes Franklin, "but we had all this great reference material. They also provided us with lightweight practical puppets that we could carry on set and use as reference. There's some amusing reference footage of me and Alex Hope, the visual effects producer and now Double Negative CEO, where we'd run out onto set with this creature balanced on our heads and run

around the set making loud clucking noises because it looked like we had this giant alien chicken on our heads! That served as our lighting reference. It actually taught me the value of absolute rock-solid reference. If you've got a photograph of what it's supposed to look like and you can point to it, then you're going to get a better result."

For Franklin, the film—which quickly gained a cult following and spawned two sequels—provided an excellent training ground for a career in visual effects. "We were mainly with the second unit team shooting nights on the stages of the studio," says Franklin. "After my full day's work wrangling things for Double Negative I'd go and shoot for a full night. So trying to find time to sleep was quite hard, but it was very exciting making it up as we went along and watching the film develop."

Batman Begins

With *Batman Begins* (2005), Paul Franklin would begin a long association with director Christopher Nolan. Here, he supervised Double Negative's monastery sequence and Gotham environment work, including a rooftop Batmobile chase and a dramatic monorail chase through the city. Franklin soon found he had high standards to meet.

"When I first met Chris Nolan on *Batman Begins*," recalls Franklin, "it was clear he was very concerned that the visual effects people might bring a certain patina of artificiality to his film that he was just totally not interested in. Chris had never used any kind of digital effects work of any form, not even digital opticals in earlier films. It was clear that Chris didn't consider any digital environment he'd seen in any movie to be of sufficient quality. He didn't want to have any distinction between the principal photography of Chicago and the work that was going to be needed to extend the city."

To provide the realism sought by Nolan, Double Negative developed a new group of techniques for how they would create the shots, starting from a photographic basis. "We came up with panoramic techniques, re-projection techniques allowing us to project the photographic imagery onto digital geometry," explains Franklin, "and we spent a lot of time working

[1] Director Christopher Nolan. **Batman Begins** represented Franklin's first collaboration with the director. "The film was entirely photochemical," notes Franklin, when referring to Nolan's love of celluloid film. "There was no digital intermediate—we were doing it all in the lab. It puts a lot of responsibility on the visual-effects people to get the grades right in their visual-effects shots."

[1]

[2] Double Negative sought to replicate the architectural details of Chicago, which was standing in for Gotham City in the film. This meant acquiring crucial panoramic and lighting references to make particular buildings and city views.

on the color pipeline in particular, so that we could faithfully reproduce the dynamic range of the film stock, and be able to grade our digital images to integrate seamlessly with our principal photography."

In addition, Franklin oversaw around 15 digital Batman double shots on the film, where shots were too difficult or unsafe to achieve as stunts. The effects required scanning the Batman suit and cloth simulation for the crusader's cape.

Franklin notes that, despite the director's initial trepidation about diving into the digital effects world,

Nolan came out trusting the effects teams to help put his vision on the screen—in fact, even more digital double and environment work, albeit invisible, would appear in the subsequent Batman movies.

"There's sometimes a fear from some filmmakers," Franklin elaborates, "that the visual effects guys are going to wander in and overwhelm them with jargon and flashy toys, and subvert their vision into something they don't want it to be. We wanted to have the best systems and a robust pipeline, but not at the expense of the creative vision of the show."

The Dark Knight and The Dark Knight Rises

Franklin would carry over key lessons he learned on *Batman Begins* to the effects for *The Dark Knight* (2008) and *The Dark Knight Rises* (2012), orchestrating further city views and destruction, digital doubles, and CG vehicles. One of those vehicles is Batman's aerial transportation—the Bat—in *The Dark Knight Rises*.

"The Bat was designed by Nathan Crowley's art department and then constructed and engineered by Chris Corbould's special effects team. Chris Nolan wanted to use the physical Bat wherever possible. The idea was that we'd get the physical thing into the shot and take it from there. The special effects team gave us access to all their digital files so we could then make a very faithful digital replica too."

The Bat was mounted on crane on top of a high-speed vehicle that could be driven along the street and maneuvered to bank and turn, with Double Negative painting out the crane and holding vehicle. More aggressive moves and flights around Gotham City then relied on a CG Bat.

"Two things made our CG version fit closely within the live-action photography," explains Franklin. "The first was the continued development of our physically based lighting system, which gave us an absolutely perfect match for the physical Bat. The animation team also spent a lot of time looking at real-world references of helicopters in action, so all the movements that the Bat does are very much based on moves that Apache helicopters can do for real. We turbo charged it a little more, though—it's traveling a lot faster than a real copter can."

Interestingly, few digital environment enhancements were required for the areas of the city the Bat weaves through. "Our previs was pretty outlandish—zooming down city canyons and all that," notes Franklin, "so I

[1] Both a practical version of the Bat Pod created by special effects supervisor Chris Corbould and a digital replica of the vehicle made by Double Negative were used in **The Dark Knight**.

[1]

[2] Double Negative carried out extensive rig removal on practical photography of the Bat, as seen in **The Dark Knight Rises**, while also generating its own CG version of the aircraft for some of the more complicated sequences.

thought no way am I going to get these as plates. But actually I was very pleasantly surprised when I arrived in Pittsburgh, where we filmed, and discovered we had extensive low flight permissions for the center of the city. Working very closely with the aerial crew I spent a week or two zooming down the streets of Pittsburgh shooting IMAX plates that we then built our sequence out of. We did one digital extension of a cityscape in that whole sequence—the rest is pretty much all live action in camera. You're trying to build the shots with the minimal amount of digital intervention. You're doing your best to base everything on some sort of observed reality rather than saying we can't shoot anything and create a fantasy land in CG."

Inception

Franklin would re-team with director Christopher Nolan, as visual effects supervisor on *Inception* (2010)—a heist movie with a difference. The dreamscapes depicted in the movie would be somewhat more fantastical than anything presented in the *Batman* films, but still grounded in reality. "It's actually a very key part of the story of *Inception*," says Franklin. "We didn't want the dreams to have any kind of tactile difference to what could be considered to be the real world portions of the film. We didn't want the dreamscape to have some kind of signature look to it. The big reveal is that you don't realize you're in the dream world under bizarre things start happening."

One of the dreamscapes Dom Cobb (Leonardo DiCaprio) shows to Ariadne (Ellen Page) features folding Paris buildings. "The concept of the folding buildings is pretty straightforward," notes Franklin. "The city has a modular look to it, so the blocks in Paris have regular floor plans even though the detail on the surface of the buildings is unique on a block-by-block basis. This suggested we could have this idea of the city rolling up

like a series of linked bridges, each of them lifting in sequence. The modules of the city would roll over and plug into ones down on the ground, effectively reflecting themselves across a common roofline."

To ensure such an initially bizarre kind of movement would also appear entirely realistic, Franklin's effects team had to add detail—and lots of it. "Detail is what the real world is," he says. "So we spent several weeks out on the location digitizing the streets, LIDAR scanning them, photographing the buildings in exquisite detail for detailed textures, and really paying attention to the reality of what happens in a real environment."

By way of example, Franklin explains: "It's so easy to make assumptions, even on simple things like the sidewalks. You might observe initially that the sidewalk is six inches high and the paving stones are three feet wide and they repeat regularly all the way down the street. Only they don't. If you look at a real sidewalk the paving stones are uneven and the curb hasn't necessarily been laid perfectly. There might be little dips in it—all this stuff goes into building up the

[1] **Inception** is notable for the wasteland-type effects in "Limbo"—the place a person ends up in if they die in a dream. Here, Double Negative relied on its destruction tools to have pieces of buildings crumbling away.

[1]

[2] Buildings in Paris fold over themselves in a dreamscape sequence from the film. Franklin visited the city and oversaw a major photography and scanning effort in order to replicate the fine details in the buildings.

character of the real environment. I have to say the team who did that for *Inception* was incredible."

The film came at a time, also, when Double Negative was making significant improvements to the way it would light CG geometry, especially for architectural environments. "The Paris street scene was the first time," says Franklin, "that we employed a physically-based approach to the lighting in order to try and reproduce the correct interplay of light, reflections, and shadows."

The effects in *Inception* have a grounding in reality, too, since many were achieved in-camera, thanks to the work of special effects supervisor Chris Corbould and his team. One such moment is the zero gravity fight in the corridor in which actors were strung on wires inside a rotating set, and for which Double Negative only had to perform minor wire removals and add floating pieces of paraphernalia. Even where some of the studio's effects

were more complicated, shooting the scenes for real provided a crucial starting point.

"The most demanding wire removals," notes Franklin, "were in the final throes of the 'kick,' when people are floating in the elevator and then slammed against the floor. There was an awful lot of re-timing and manipulation of the bodies to make it look like they were slamming into the floor. We had them hanging vertically and we were bringing the carpet up against them—not too hard—but to make it feel like an impact was happening. Little moments like that tend to take a long time to do."

6 > Karen Goulekas

Before Karen Goulekas became a visual-effects artist and then a supervisor on films such as *Godzilla*, *The Day After Tomorrow*, *10,000 BC*, and *Green Lantern*, she had not considered a career as an artist, and instead pursued journalism. "I can't draw to save my life," she admits. "The last time I took an art course I spent a lot of time doing a pen-and-ink drawing in the 8th grade and when I turned it in I got a D. I was told 'stick with writing.'"

After gaining some experience in broadcasting, Goulekas soon became an expert in early on-screen graphics and animation equipment for broadcast in the mid 1980s, using a computer called the Dubner. "They plunked that thing down in front of me," she recalls, "and I'd never touched a computer! All of a sudden if I just made a cube it was in the correct 3D perspective, and I couldn't believe it. It was like, 'Oh my God I can make pretty pictures, even though I'd been told my whole life I can't make images.'"

"My husband was working in Boston," adds Goulekas, "and when I looked for a job there, there was only one Dubner in the whole town and they already had a Dubner artist. But I heard she was giving notice, so I went up there and they said, 'You know how to use a Dubner?' I had my reel right there and they said, 'Don't go anywhere!' It was such a rare thing and they looked at my reel and I was hired on the spot."

Goulekas continued honing her animation skills while she carried out assignments in Boston and New York, including at NBC for the Barcelona Summer Olympics. Then Goulekas saw James Cameron's *Terminator 2: Judgment Day* in 1991. "I remember going to that movie and feeling sick to my stomach because I was like, 'Those effects are jaw dropping and what the hell am I doing sitting here making kitty litter commercials?' It hit me that if I didn't get out to California and get into the film market there then I would miss out."

Armed with a demo reel, Goulekas scored a three-month stint at Boss Films in Los Angeles doing commercial work and was asked to stay on. She never returned to the east coast. "I called my husband and said, 'You realize I'm not coming back, pack the house!'"

Goulekas moved on to more feature film effects at the brand new Digital Domain studio created by James Cameron, Stan Winston, and Scott Ross, where she contributed to such films as *True Lies*, *Apollo 13*, and *The Fifth Element*. "I think I was artist number ten at Digital Domain," says Goulekas, "and that's really where I got a film education. I moved up the ranks to be digital effects supervisor."

On *The Fifth Element*, in particular, Goulekas convinced the overall supervisors that previs would be a key factor in devising the city car chase sequence, as it would combine both miniature buildings and digital vehicles. For the CG cars, ray tracing techniques that might be used today for the optimum photorealistic rendering of metallic surfaces were then (around 1996) both expensive and time consuming. "Instead," says Goulekas, "we used similar tricks that are used on set to adjust lighting. We would place random black-and-white cards outside the camera view as part of the reflection mapping to get a more real world feel. It helped, but let's face it—it's not easy to fake ray tracing."

Goulekas would leave Digital Domain to become an independent supervisor on *Godzilla*, released in 1998. She has remained an independent VFX supervisor ever since and in addition to *The Day After Tomorrow*, *10,000 BC*, and *Green Lantern*, her credits include *Spider-Man*, *Eight Legged Freaks*, and *Looper*.

Looper, in particular, is a project Goulekas says she really enjoyed, as it was not "an in-your-face effects film like some I've worked on. It was my first indie film from start to finish and so I got to wear all the different hats—data wrangling, producing, co-ordinating, and supervising. I enjoyed it because it kind of got me back into the trenches."

[1] Karen Goulekas. Image courtesy of Karen Goulekas.

[2] Leeloo (Milla Jovovich)
finds herself in a precarious
position in **The Fifth Element**.
Goulekas was a digital-
effects supervisor at Digital
Domain on the film.

Godzilla

Goulekas' first independent visual-effects supervision role away from an individual studio was on Roland Emmerich's *Godzilla* (1998). Here, she came onto the production as an associate visual-effects supervisor to work with overall supervisor Volker Engel with eight months of post-production remaining. "I met Roland and he was such a great guy and we had a fantastic time working together," she says. "It was the first time I'd really felt like I was one of the filmmakers. It really felt like moviemaking. But it was also probably the hardest I'd worked in my life. I was like, 'Oh my God, I'm either going to fry in the frying pan and go down with this or I've gotta pull it all out.'"

"I'd do walkthroughs at Centropolis Effects, where we were based, at 8am and we'd still be doing rounds at the other facilities at 2am or 3am," notes Goulekas on the intense workload required. "It was the days when you didn't have high-resolution playback machines to see all the details and everyone FTPing their shots to you. So, literally, I'd go twice a day to all the facilities and we'd get calls at 2am saying, 'Are you guys still coming over?' and we'd go, 'Oh, we'll be there in 30 minutes.'" The film's central character, Godzilla, and its interaction with New York streetscapes was achieved with a mix of practical, miniature, and (at the time) groundbreaking CG creature effects. One initial approach considered by the filmmakers was to use motion capture for Godzilla—essentially a person wearing a mocap suit that would be re-targeted to match the creature's walk cycle. But when Goulekas came on the film she quickly realized motion capture could not adequately make Godzilla move like the giant lizard he needed to be, so a mostly keyframe animation solution was settled upon.

Another sequence Goulekas supervised involved Godzilla crossing the Brooklyn Bridge. "I came in and again they were talking about doing motion capture," she says. "They built a beautiful miniature bridge—I saw it and it was gorgeous, but I said, 'Well what are we going to do with that?' And they said they were going to shake it and twist it for when Godzilla runs over it. And I said, 'Wait that's not going to work—the bridge is going to have to move relative to his steps and the weight of him.' If they were just shaking it, first of all we couldn't camera track it in those days, and how would it correspond to his footsteps? So I determined we had to do it all CG, which was a really scary statement to make.

[1] The creature chases a taxi cab onto the Brooklyn Bridge. A number of approaches were considered for the bridge shot, including a man in a suit, a miniature bridge, motion capture, and a fully digital scene, the latter being the chosen method.

[2] Godzilla thunders through the streets of New York. This CG version of the monster was crafted by artists at Centropolis Effects based on original concepts by creature designer Patrick Tatopoulos.

I remember on *The Fifth Element* having some fully CG city stuff and how long it took to do."

Of course, in the end the shot was done with a fully CG Godzilla and bridge, which rocks and rolls as Godzilla runs—which also causes a bunch of snapping cables and a crumbling road underfoot. Goulekas credits the

success of that sequence, too, on her instigation that the shots should be previs'd first as a blueprint for the whole scene. "Everybody was nervous about it, myself included, but I didn't see a better way to get it done. It helps that it's at night and raining. The team did a great job on that."

The Day After Tomorrow

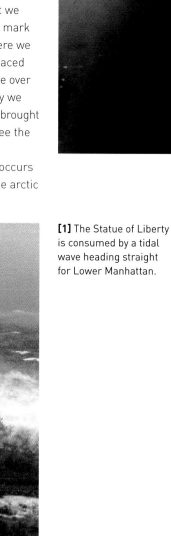

Goulekas re-teamed with Emmerich as the visual-effects supervisor on *The Day After Tomorrow* (2004), a film that portrays the result of a sudden global cooling and subsequent ice age. To depict various disruptive weather events, Goulekas would need to oversee the creation of tidal waves, mass flooding, ice and snow effects, destructive twisters, and even wolves.

After pushing the director toward previs in *Godzilla*, Goulekas again took that route on this new disaster adventure, even utilizing low-resolution geometry of New York from a third-party provider to help flesh out how parts of the city would be flooded. "Roland became a big fan of CG and previs," she recalls. "He said let's get a team in there early. He knew what he wanted. And out of previs we came up with other ideas."

While water effects were clearly something that could be done digitally, Goulekas says that at the time "water was still hard. Some of the water simulations just took such a long time, and we needed to get the movie out!"

The long simulation times were partly the result of adhering closely to what the pure physics of a tidal wave or a wave careening through a New York street would look like. Instead, Goulekas needed the water to be more art-directable. "We'd always start with what real physics would be if we had a big wave coming through our city," explains Goulekas. "Then it might not work in the cut, like a big wave would happen too soon or it would happen on a street where we didn't want it. And that's where the real art came in. First it was hard for the programmers to write a real physical sim, but then because we were making a movie, we'd say well this is cool, this is reality, but we'd art direct it to make the wave hit 30 frames earlier and we'd want it to be on this building and not that building."

A major effects sequence in the film sees multiple twisters wreaking havoc in Los Angeles. "For that we gathered tons of reference," says Goulekas. "We'd mark our favorite twisters and we'd do an animatic where we took those favorites and cut them out and then placed them in the live-action plates. We'd say, 'I want one over here that's a double twister like this one.' Literally we had floating video bits of twisters, so that when we brought it over to the visual effects company they would see the type of twister that we wanted."

One of the film's most memorable sequences occurs under the opening titles—a two-and-a-half minute arctic

[1] The Statue of Liberty is consumed by a tidal wave heading straight for Lower Manhattan.

[2] Twisters spring up in Los Angeles. Digital Domain, the visual effects studio behind these tornadoes, built a "twister toolkit" to mix and match volumetric pieces to form the final creations.

fly-over completed entirely in CG. At the time, the 4,000 frame shot was believed to be one of the longest all-digital shots created for a film. Interestingly, it was also an effect that would later stir up controversy in the debate about global warming when Al Gore used the fly-over footage (minus the title credits) in his 2006 film *An Inconvenient Truth*.

"After *The Day After Tomorrow* came out," recounts Goulekas, "somebody did an article about how the film's effects would really happen. And a camera crew from 20/20 came to my house to do an interview about the film, and the funny thing is I hadn't seen the Gore video and it was our opening scene and I said we had created that in the computer. This became a big thing, a huge thing, with reports saying 'Karen Goulekas admits that global warming is fake!' But all I said was that particular shot is computer generated, based on real footage that we had referenced."

10,000 BC

By this point in her career, Goulekas had done her fair share of disaster flicks. Roland Emmerich's prehistoric adventure film, *10,000 BC* (2008), was certainly a change of pace, but still a massive visual effects challenge. "This wasn't any easier," Goulekas admits. "We still had to do convincing wet fur for the sabertooth cat and long hair on the mammoths, and we had a lot of complex environments and crowd shots too."

Still, Goulekas describes her work on the film as the best shooting experience she's ever had. "What made it so good was the fact that we got to shoot in New Zealand, South Africa, and Namibia. The highlight was when the whole crew had to camp for two weeks in Namibia—the same location for the opening of *2001: A Space Odyssey*."

"There were no hotels in any direction for two hours," says Goulekas, "so they set up military tents for 500 crew members. It was just amazing. They built a bar too. At the end of the day the entire crew would be in this bar on the desert! We had signs all over to make sure to shine a flashlight in the toilet at night because snakes would come up the toilets. I won't ever have another experience like that again."

Digital mammoths were one of the first CG creations contemplated by the visual effects supervisor. Among the challenges were the different lengths of mammoth hair and the way it would interact when entangled with human nets—effects that visual effects studio MPC would spend months researching and developing. A view of the mammoths on the pyramid ramp would also be one with significant planning required.

"We knew we'd have hundreds of extras running on that ramp," says Goulekas. "I was thinking, how are we going to keep the extras from running where the mammoths should be? We decided to make a base with wheels on it that represented the width and length of

[1] The mammoths haul bricks along the pyramid ramp. Different views of these shots involved shooting miniatures and also filming with just mammoth cut-outs so that extras did not run into the paths of the animals that would be achieved digitally.

[2] The sabertooth cat threatens D'Leh (Steven Strait) in a water pit. Double Negative combined both fur and fluid simulations to create this sequence.

the form of the mammoths. We ended up making a true scale mammoth cut-out that was blue but was more like netting. There were high winds up there so they said it was dangerous to have anything that could get knocked over—the holes allowed wind to go through it. We had that for eyelines as well as this massive thing to move around so the extras wouldn't run through it."

For the sabertooth cat—a creature that would be realized by Double Negative—a full-sized print of the tiger was made and tied to scaffolding. "We would have our data wranglers walking with it through the set so our camera operators and actors could rehearse eyelines and where the camera needed to be," says Goulekas. "The funniest thing was that we had a lot of tribal

members who were extras," adds Goulekas. "When one of them saw our data wranglers walking through with just a print of our tiger, he walked up to the producer and said, 'I don't think anyone's going to believe that's a real tiger.' He thought we were using it as a real take!"

Further creatures required for the film included terror birds, completed by Double Negative, which needed to fight a group of hunters. "For those we basically built a true-sized terror bird head and put it on sticks," explains Goulekas. "So the actor had to whack the bird knowing it was really just papier-mâché. The people holding the sticks were all dressed in blue leotards and that was good comedy watching guys in leotards running around waving blue bird heads."

Green Lantern

Glowing green suits, alien creatures, interstellar environments, and an amorphous cloud of evil skulls called Parallax—these were just some of the visual effects requirements faced by Goulekas on Martin Campbell's telling of the DC Comics character film *Green Lantern* (2011).

Principal vendor Sony Pictures Imageworks delivered, in particular, hundreds of effects shots for test pilot Hal Jordan's (Ryan Reynolds) green suit after he unwittingly becomes a member of the intergalactic Green Lantern Corps. The suit was rendered as all-digital, so on set Reynolds would wear a gray tracking suit and sometimes make-up tracking markers for when he had to sport a green mask. In addition to the principal film camera, the actor was also filmed with two witness cameras that would help in tracking his relative position in the frame in order to place him in a CG suit.

The suit featured a constant flow of energy running inside and emanating from it, but, perhaps surprisingly, Goulekas highlights the interaction between the CG suit and the actor's neck as the hardest part of bringing the character to life. "The neck has so much motion, if you think about the way the skin twists and turn," she says. "You really have to be able to extract that and track it. If that CG suit doesn't move the same way the neck is moving, the whole gag is given away. We had used a facial action coding system, or FACS, to capture the poses—Imageworks dubbed it NACS instead, for neck animation poses!"

Jordan inherits the ability to fly, a stunt achieved both by hanging Reynolds from wires against a bluescreen, and also by creating the character (and others who fly with him) as CG models. "I put a shooting bible together of types of flying shots," says Goulekas, "where I would say we want the actor on a belly pan, or a bluescreen actor, or this type of a shot can be full CG. Imageworks would tell me it was sometimes easier to do him full CG flying by than to shoot him and do the tracking and suit and get the interaction working."

As the *Green Lantern*, Jordan is able to conjure almost any kind of object or weapon, known as a construct. Reynolds would mimic holding, say a Gatling gun, in the shot that Imageworks would later complete as a glowing and semi-transparent green creation.

For Parallax—an organic mass of souls in the form of skull and skeleton tendrils that grows as it takes over planets on its way to Earth—the visual effects team had to do further R&D, especially for the complex volumetrics surrounding the character. "They almost treated that like a cloth simulation," comments Goulekas. "It had to be based on a simulation, but then you had to be able to adjust it. I wanted, say, that space in there to be able to scream at this moment. And I wanted that skull to go flying out."

"I always say," adds Goulekas, "don't rely 100 percent on a simulation because you're going to need to do some hand work. That same thing goes for motion capture, for example, because you're always going to want to change the timing and speed. A lot of times people are hoping one will cancel out the other, but you really still need the artists."

[1] Hal Jordan (Ryan Reynolds) becomes Green Lantern. A major component of the Lantern character was his digital green suit, which had layers of muscle shapes and skin built into it to replicate a human body.

[3]

[2] Parallax attacks. Sony Pictures Imageworks relied on a proprietary volumetric renderer to help realize the tendril-like structures and diaphanous tissue surfaces of the creature.

[3] The Green Lantern Corps character Tomar-Re (voiced by Geoffrey Rush)— a completely CG creation.

7 > Ian Hunter

Model and miniature effects supervisor Ian Hunter began his career as a model maker on possibly one of the most influential effects films in history—James Cameron's *The Abyss*. "I came in and was given a set of dimensions (10-feet long x 5-feet wide x 3-feet tall) and told to make a submarine engine room. No plans, no drawings, just figure it out and go. So myself and a great model maker named Jim McGeachy grabbed a piece of paper and sketched out what we thought a submarine engine room should look like, based on that size and James' request to have a walkway down the middle. We then started building it. We knew it would be flooded so we built it from waterproof materials and made it pretty durable to withstand being dropped in the water. Not a bad way to get introduced into the business."

Hunter is now a partner—with Matthew Gratzner and Shannon Blake Ganns—at New Deal Studios, a powerhouse miniature, practical, and visual effects company in Hollywood. Formerly Hunter/Gratzner Industries, the studio is responsible for key buildings, vehicles, explosions, and effects in films such as *Alien: Resurrection*, *Godzilla*, *The X-Files*, *Pitch Black*, *The Aviator*, *Live Free or Die Hard*, *The Dark Knight*, *The Dark Knight Rises*, *Shutter Island*, *Inception*, *Hugo*, and *Interstellar* (for which Hunter won an Oscar for achievement in visual effects).

Once synonymous with miniatures, New Deal Studios has evolved to become a full service studio, offering practical and digital effects work and technical previs. "What we are always striving for at New Deal Studios is to provide memorable, high-quality images, iconic shots that make the scene," says Hunter. "I think we differ from others out in the visual effects field because we understand what we are providing is part of the whole movie experience. We've had a director stand up in a meeting and say he wanted us on his movie, not because we were model makers, but because we were filmmakers. We get movies."

Hunter says creating believable miniature effects shots involves many factors. "First and foremost is how will the miniature be used? Will it need to sit there and look believable like a landscape or a building, or will it need to do something, like burn or blow up or go through a stunt? The function of the miniature affects its

scale—the size the model is built—and what it is made of. If the miniature will be seen from a distance then the scale of the model can be reduced. The closer you need to get with the model, the larger the scale should be, so factors such as materials, textures, and paint can hold up to scrutiny the closer you get to the model."

"When a miniature has to function—explode, burn, break—then the scales will increase and the models will get bigger," continues Hunter. "Certain properties like breaking and sliding objects or destruction with explosives can scale down well, but will need to be shot at a high frame rate, so that when the resulting action is slowed down to a normal frame rate the movement of the material has apparent weight and mass. Physical factors like water and flame do not scale as well, and the miniatures used for water interaction or sustained burning need to be built in a larger scale, so that the size of flame licks or water drops become believable."

"Sometimes an overall miniature might be built in one scale to get the detail and lighting for a scene, but then larger scale elements can be added to enhance believability," says Hunter. "Models that get destroyed need to be made of breakaway materials that can be scored or broken easily. Pyro explosives should only be used to create the 'look' of the explosion, with air mortars or cable ratchets being used to yank parts and expand the effect."

Hunter says one of his favorite projects to date was David Twohy's *Pitch Black* (2000) when the company was

known as Hunter/Gratzner Industries: "Matthew and myself got to sit in a room together with the director and work out how to depict the crash of the spaceship at the beginning of the movie. Those meetings with David affected the design of the ship, which Matthew did, and the shot design, which I got to storyboard. It really allowed us to build shots for a scene that we knew was going to cut together and work because of the preliminary work done with David. The frosting on the cake for *Pitch Black* was the spaceship that crashes was named the Hunter/Gratzner."

[3]

The X-Files

The popular Fox series *The X-Files* made the jump from television to the movie screen with the 1998 movie, *The X-Files*, directed by Rob Bowman. A crucial establishing scene was the detonation of a federal building in Dallas, as Fox Mulder (David Duchovny) and Dana Scully (Gillian Anderson) are investigating a bomb threat there. Hunter/Gratzner Industries constructed and destroyed a scale miniature of the building for the scene.

"Even though *The X-Files* is science fiction," relates Hunter, "it deals with its subject matter in the same way as a straight drama, so the explosion scene had to play out as real. We actually studied building demolition footage and the tragic Oklahoma City Federal Building explosion to see what kind of things happen to a building during a collapse."

Real location photographs taken from the shoot in downtown Los Angeles by the film's visual effects supervisor, Mat Beck, were also referenced, as Hunter/Gratzner would be matching the building exactly. They also looked to previs of the scene delivered from Beck. "Interestingly," says Hunter, "this was not a huge budget film, so we could not actually construct the full building pristine and then destroy it. Instead, we built the miniature 'pre-disastered,' with broken floors and damaged walls. We then built a central finished section of the building wall that we could get a close-up on to give the impression in the cut that the building starts out intact."

The construction process for the miniature began with the erection of a steel frame and drywall-covered wall that would absorb the fire and explosions. "We calculated the sun angle for the day and the time we planned to shoot, and set the model up in a large vacant lot at a particular angle to get the lighting to match," explains Hunter. "The floors were on air rams that could retract to let the floor fall and drop pre-broken debris. Pyro cannon and air mortars hidden behind the model and firing out of narrow slots at the base created flames and a pyroclastic-type billowing cloud of debris."

For the finished center wall, artists hung the section from the pre-disastered main building. Then the finished wall was cut into a radiating series of pieces, held together with thin lines of monofilament. "Each piece had its own filament," notes Hunter. "By placing little explosive squibs on the lines we could sequence the explosions and drop the pieces of the wall in order from bottom to top, center to outside, so it looked like the main explosion was radiating out from the bottom center. This part of the model only worked from the one high camera looking down."

A large mortar with a fireball then exploded at the base of the building, right as the wall pieces fell into the flames. A fireball consuming the camera lens was designed into the shot. "This allows a cut to a wide shot that shows the remainder of the wall collapsing," says Hunter. "We also put a weak knee under the roof so it could collapse. Another fireball at the base of the building explodes and crawls up the face of the pre-disastered building, allowing overlapping action between the first shot and second."

The stunning explosion shots, which were composited into wide views of the location, also included an angle of the actors walking up to the building. "This was duplicated with a motion-controlled panning camera that we did as an aftermath shot," says Hunter. "Small fluttering government papers come floating down during the shot, courtesy of me and two assistants pushing cut-up phone book pages off of the roof with brooms."

[1] The Federal Building model in "pre-disastered" form, positioned against bluescreen so that it can be composited into final shots.

The Dark Knight

To help tell the second part of his Batman trilogy, *The Dark Knight* (2008), director Christopher Nolan looked to digital, makeup, practical, and miniature effects. New Deal Studios was tapped, in particular, to create model vehicles and a tunnel location for a scene in which Harvey Dent (Aaron Eckhart) is in an armored car being chased by the Joker (Heath Ledger) and his henchmen who are driving a garbage truck.

"The garbage truck is bearing down," describes Hunter, "and just then the armored car swerves out of the way because the Batmobile is speeding at them. The garbage truck and Batmobile crash head on. Nolan wanted to have the Batmobile smash into the garbage truck and just keep going without stopping. Now, the garbage truck was larger than the Batmobile, so we called the players 'David and Goliath.' We had to find a way to get the truck to instantly stop and then get driven back by the smaller Batmobile—you know, defy the laws of physics!"

New Deal's challenges on the sequence extended to matching plate photography filmed in Chicago and the actual picture cars used for other shots, including the Batmobile devised by special effects supervisor Chris Corbould. "One of the first things we did was go to the location in Chicago where they were shooting the real truck and Batmobile, and photograph the heck out of them and the underground road location so we could match it as closely as possible, down to the rust stains on the garbage truck's bumpers," says Hunter. "We then modeled the location and vehicles in 3D to create construction drawings and previs the action."

"Another thing we wanted to make sure of," adds Hunter, "was to photograph the models in a way that would allow the model shots to intercut with the live action seamlessly. They had shot the live action from Scorpions—Mercedes Benz SUVs with roof-mounted camera cranes. We created our own 1/3-scale versions using rock 'n' roll truss, a go-cart chassis, a motion controlled jib arm, and motion-controllable Libra camera heads. Because the cameras were moving and the vehicles were driving we had to build the set quite long to account for run up and coverage of the action. At the far end of the miniature set we used a classic

[1]

[1] Michael Caine as Alfred walks past the Batmobile in **The Dark Knight**. Ian Hunter's team at New Deal Studios would meticulously match the vehicle in miniature for a dramatic truck chase and crash sequence in then film.

[2] The Batmobile, or Tumbler. New Deal Studios referenced photography filmed in Chicago and actual picture cars used for othershots in their miniature work.

trick—we made a photo-blowup backing of the underground road and added diminishing Christmas lights to look like receding streetlights."

The matching model-sized camera cars, garbage truck, and Batmobile were then pulled through the set on cables mounted underneath through slots in the roadway. "These cables were in turn driven by computer controlled servo motors," explains Hunter, "so that all the vehicles could be driven and their actions choreographed together."

Goliath—the garbage truck—was purposefully built out of lightweight aluminum and foil with plastic resin, while the Batmobile had a thick fiberglass shell built over a steel plate body and chassis. "That way," says Hunter, "the Batmobile was actually more massive than the garbage truck, even though it was smaller."

Under the set, a large hydraulic shock absorber was attached below the Batmobile. This hit the below-deck

trolley that pulled the garbage truck before the truck and Batmobile collided on the roadway. "The shock absorber took out most of the force and speed of the garbage truck," notes Hunter, "so the Batmobile—using a steel knife edge plow up front—could lift the truck up and smash it into the ceiling without slowing down. With this system we could get the Batmobile to hit the garbage truck and have the truck's roof smash into the ceiling of the tunnel within a two-foot mark—not bad for four objects moving at different speeds within a 120-foot long set!"

Hunter continues that, "Because of the repeatability in the drive and shooting system, and the fact that we built spare garbage truck bodies, we could shoot the effect multiple times if needed. We got the shot that's in the movie on the first take."

The Dark Knight Rises

[1]

Hunter returned to work on Christopher's Nolan's follow-up to *The Dark Knight* with further miniatures work for the opening sequence to *The Dark Knight Rises* (2012). Here, an Embraer twin turboprop aircraft carrying a Russian nuclear scientist and the mercenary Bane (Tom Hardy) is chased down by a larger C-130 military Hercules and boarded by Bane's men. "Out of the C-130 bad guys rappel on lines and land on the Embraer," describes Hunter. "This was done for real! They attach cables to the fuselage and then the C-130 pulls ahead and flips the Embraer over."

Aerial photography of the Embraer and C-130 was shot over Scotland, with Hunter and New Deal Studios stepping in to provide miniature practical effects for the flipping shot and the wings being torn off the smaller plane. "We built a large-scale copy of the Embraer," says Hunter. "We used photographs and the previs model of the plane to remodel the plane in 3D. Then we used this digital model to CNC cut patterns of the plane, which were molded and cast in fiberglass. This way we could match the miniature to the full-sized plane."

In New Deal's backlot, the finished miniature was mounted to cables from above, similar to a marionette puppet. "Using separate pull cables connected to air rams, we could flip the plane over," explains Hunter.

"The wings and tail planes of the Embraer were pre-scored and broken. Cable cutters and explosive primer cord were installed within the wings and tail, which were mounted to their own set of pull cables connected to individual air rams."

"It was important to Christopher Nolan that it look like the wings were being torn off from wind buffeting and not explosives," adds Hunter. "So we only used the primer cord to cut the wing pieces, not create any flash or fire. We shot the plane outdoors in sunlight against a giant greenscreen (to be composited into the live-action aerial plates) with a moving camera that matched the motion of the aerial background plate shot in Scotland."

For maximum control of the events, including the flip, engine burn-out, and the ripping of the wings, New Deal choreographed the timings from a digital control box. The shots were captured at 72 frames per second over two days—the studio created two copies of the plane to provide, as Hunter describes, "two bites at the apple."

[1] The Dark Knight Rises
director Christopher Nolan
on the set during filming.
A key scene in the film's
prologue featuring Bane
and his adversaries hijacking
another aircraft and a nuclear
scientist would make use
of Nolan's trademark
combination of live action,
digital, and miniature effects.

Inception

Between *The Dark Knight* films, Hunter also worked with Christopher Nolan on *Inception* (2010), building and destroying the fortress hospital, a giant concrete-and-steel building perched on the edge of a snow-covered peak. "It was something worthy of the most bad-ass Bond villain's lair," says Hunter. "Also, in true Christopher Nolan fashion he asked for it to be destroyed in a very spectacular, but challenging, manner. Because the collapse of the hospital also relates to the collapse of the dream world the characters of the movie are in, Christopher did not want the fortress to just 'blow up.' Rather, he wanted to see it collapse and disintegrate, with pieces falling apart over a protracted period, starting at the front tower of the complex and finishing at the large back building."

To facilitate that kind of meticulous destruction for what—in reality— would be a very strong structure, New Deal Studios devised new materials and techniques to bring the fortress down. "We started by working with the visual effects company on the show, Double Negative, to previs the scene, and we used the previs to set up a sequence of events that would take down the fortress. I went to the location in Calgary to measure and photograph the partial live-action set that Guy Dyas' team had built—which was still a huge set perched on the side of a snow covered mountain peak!"

"With the previs and photos of the set," continues Hunter, "and a partial 3D model of the fortress, my art department set about creating a digital version of the fortress complex to build from. We actually calculated the sun angle for the time and day we planned on shooting the model and angled the set in our backlot so that the sun would be coming in at just the right angle to match with the lighting in Calgary."

Since the collapsing fortress was supposed to crumble continuously, Hunter chose to "bypass gravity" for the primary collapse—this simply meant the effects artists would control the rate of the fall. "We built collapsible steel frames controlled by hydraulic rams that the main buildings attached to," says Hunter. "Each individual floor section of each building had its own steel support structure that we attached the model walls to

and these structures could be released in a specific sequence using cable releases mounted to another hydraulic controlled structure we called 'the harp.'"

Materials for the fortress had to look like concrete, but be fragile and be able to break away. "For that," explains Hunter, "we came up with a method of casting parts with a sprayed thin plaster skin, but with a weak urethane foam backing. These fragile parts could be scored and pre-broken, attached to the steel structure, and lifted in place on our mountain peak with a crane. It was like putting together a 47-foot tall Faberge egg."

New Deal then consulted the live action explosions that special effects supervisor Chris Corbould had orchestrated, matching these on the 1/6-scale model for color, texture, and size. "Christopher Nolan considers effects shots to be like any other shot in his movie," notes Hunter, "so he prefers that the event action be shot in its entirety from beginning to end to allow it to be edited and intercut. So the whole fortress complex collapse had to be filmed as one long event, covered with five cameras, including one done as a 'helicopter' flyover—a remote head on a Technocrane held up 70 feet in the air by a construction crane."

Digital timers set the explosions, floor drops, and building collapses, with New Deal capturing the shots in two takes. "Overall there were some 200 events happening during the collapse," says Hunter. "I used a video monitor image of the helicopter shot to line up a position to start the event, and gladly pushed the button that started the explosions. After 14 weeks of planning and construction, we did the first take. The event was over in an actual 5.5 seconds. We filmed the shot at 72 frames per second, which gave us 16.5 seconds of screen time from beginning to end."

[1] Dom Cobb (Leonardo DiCaprio) and Ariadne (Ellen Page) in the hospital fortress at the conclusion of **Inception**. Wide shots of the fortress as it collapses were achieved via New Deal Studios miniatures overseen by Ian Hunter.

8 > John Knoll

John Knoll understands imagery. Not only is he an experienced senior visual effects supervisor at Industrial Light & Magic (ILM), but along with his brother Thomas, he is also one of he co-creators of Adobe Photoshop. Knoll became ILM's Chief Creative Officer in 2013 after starting with the studio in the mid-1980s as a motion control camera assistant.

Knoll's credit list includes *Baby's Day Out*, *Star Trek: Generations*, *Mission: Impossible*, *Star Trek: First Contact*, the *Star Wars* prequel trilogy, *Mission to Mars*, the first three *Pirates of the Caribbean* films, *Avatar*, *Rango*, *Mission: Impossible—Ghost Protocol*, and *Pacific Rim*. Knoll's work on *Pirates of the Caribbean: Dead Man's Chest*, which starred the break-through digital Davy Jones character, earned the visual effects supervisor an Academy Award—he's been nominated a further four times.

[1]

Although his beginnings were in miniatures, motion control, and optical camera effects, Knoll quickly became a digital advocate at ILM—he thought computer graphics could have a much larger role in visual effects. This was driven by his experience with Photoshop (initially called "Display") and observations of the Lucasfilm Computer Division's specialized Pixar Image Computer—that division was ultimately spun off to form Pixar Animation Studios. "Actually, it was George Lucas who was frustrated by the limits of what could be done with optical printing then," says Knoll. "The whole concept of an optical printer was a camera being pointed into a projector to re-photograph elements. To do anything of any complexity was this giant logistical nightmare and it wasn't interactive. You couldn't tell what you were really getting until you saw it developed the next day. For all you knew you might have made a silly mistake three steps into a 300-step process."

"To have computers assist in the process really seemed like the future," adds Knoll. "As soon as I got a demo of the Pixar Image Computer, that for me was like a light bulb going off. I thought, 'Oh my God, that's the future—that's going to change everything.'"

Certainly, ILM revolutionized the visual effects industry with its use of computer graphics, particularly on films like *The Abyss*, *Terminator 2: Judgment Day*, and *Jurassic Park*. At that point, though, Knoll observed that the studio had been able to make organic creatures

well, but that "hard surface" assets were not necessarily going through its pipeline in the most efficient manner.

Knoll took it upon himself to experiment with some of the new, commercially available and easier-to-use CG tools, including the increasingly popular Electric Image. "I was playing around with these lower-end tools on consumer workstations," he says. "I thought we could perhaps do some simpler jobs a lot more cost effectively with them. I did some animatics and shot design on *Baby's Day Out* in Electric Image. Then on *Star Trek: Generations* I did some finished shots using the software. Most of the shots of the Enterprise in that movie were of the six-foot long model filmed on the motion-control stage. There was one required shot in particular, though, of the Enterprise going into warp drive and it seemed like the right way to do this was computer graphics as the ship elongates and stretches. So I thought I'm going to try doing this Enterprise shot myself using desktop tools. And that's the shot that's in the movie."

Having worked on creatures and effects ranging from giant robots to elaborate space battles, Knoll has also delivered scores of more "invisible" effects sequences. "There's tremendous fun to be had in the big, broad, robot-smashing-a-building kind of stuff," he admits. "It is very bold, in-your-face kind of work, but there's no mistaking you're looking at something synthetic. But the invisible stuff is really fun to work on as well—if you do it right, nobody knows you've done anything."

[1] John Knoll in his office at Industrial Light & Magic in San Francisco.

[2] Davy Jones (Bill Nighy) in **Pirates of the Caribbean: Dead Man's Chest**. Nighy wore a gray tracking suit on set that ILM would use along with high-definition cameras and its iMocap system to animate the character.

Sometimes the need for invisible effects work can come from surprising circumstances, such as on *Mission: Impossible—Ghost Protocol*, when Knoll's team had to create a CG version of a BMW i8 concept car as it speeds through the streets of Mumbai. "We shot for one evening of what was supposed to be a week-long shoot with the real car," relates Knoll. "But on the first setup of the second day we broke the transmission and it couldn't be repaired. Then all of a sudden it was, 'Well, the car's broken and it needs to be a CG car now.' Right away we had to leap into action and organize a target car and tracking markers, and then scan the car and do our digital version. It's always fun to show the befores and afters on that because people go, 'Oh my God, you're kidding me!'"

Mission: Impossible

Knoll brought both his model making and digital effects sensibilities to the fore in Brian De Palma's *Mission: Impossible* (1996), particularly for a daring end sequence in which Ethan Hunt is pursued on a train through the Channel Tunnel that links England to France. Exterior views featured a CG helicopter and train built by ILM, with bluescreen elements of Hunt fighting Jim Phelps (Jon Voight) on top of the moving train. Inside the tunnel a mix of CG assets, as well as 1/8-scale miniature environments, and train and helicopter models rigged to explode were used—with actors performing on wires and rigs against a bluescreen.

The resulting final sequence was a strong indication of ILM's ability to combine miniatures and digital elements. But the complex shots also required careful planning. Traditionally, filmmakers used storyboards to set out scenes, but there had also been a more advanced use of animatics and previs—something Knoll was aching to do after an experience on an earlier movie.

"On *Star Trek: Generations*," recalls Knoll, "we had a scene in the space dock—the opening scene where the Enterprise is being christened. My art director on that had drawn a composition that looked great and everybody loved, and then when he got it onto the stage we couldn't

[1] Tom Cruise as Ethan Hunt, filming a scene for the movie **Mission: Impossible** in a studio, 1995. In this scene he clings to a replica of a TGV train built on the set, against a bluescreen.

[1]

[2] Tom Cruise is propelled toward the moving train by the explosion of the helicopter. For this shot, Cruise was swung on a wire against a bluescreen, with ILM adding in the explosion elements based on miniature models and pyrotechnics.

get that angle. So while the drawing was well rendered, it wasn't 'perspective-correct.' He had inadvertently made the size of the dish relative to other elements not technically correct. It was a very frustrating experience out on the stage to have this composition that was approved, but that we couldn't get."

"I swore after that experience that I wasn't going to rely on drawn storyboards for important compositional things anymore," adds Knoll. "Early on I was going to move to doing things in perspective correct 3D. About a third of the way into that show I started building simple CG models of a lot of the assets and I would do shot design in 3D so then I'd know for sure that any shot I designed would be correct."

When *Mission: Impossible* came along, Knoll initially worked with De Palma to storyboard the train and helicopter chase. "About a month before we went into the stage to shoot all the bluescreen elements for that scene," says Knoll, "Brian said he wanted a list of all the camera focal lengths and positions, so there was no guessing on the stage. It seemed like the natural way to do that was to have a CG model of the train and helicopter, and layout those shots in perspective-correct 3D. I did a first pass on that and then, after I had done stills reproducing the storyboards, Brian requested running footage with animatics. This was just like a previs, and it worked tremendously in helping us make the sequence."

[3] Tom Cruise clings to a helicopter strut against a bluescreen during filming for the train sequence.

Star Wars: Episode I—The Phantom Menace

Among the many challenges in George Lucas' *Star Wars: Episode I—The Phantom Menace* (1999) was the Boonta Eve podrace on Tatooine, in which a young Anakin Skywalker (Jake Lloyd) proves his skills as a pilot. The sequence would showcase the race using aerial views, in-pod shots, and views close to the—often destructive—action. Whilst the pods would be CG creations, Knoll wanted to explore a range of options for the environments they pass through.

Knoll firstly considered shooting aerial plates from a helicopter, but soon determined that the pods would be traveling faster than a helicopter could fly and that over-cranking the camera would make the plates appear jerky. "Frankly," he adds, "the real landscapes around the world weren't exotic enough for what George had come up with. Even if they did exist, we were flying through these very narrow confines and under arches —it wouldn't have been practical with real terrain."

[1] Anakin Skywalker's pod races through the Tatooine desert.

[1]

[2] Podrace backgrounds were achieved with multiple techniques, including miniatures, CG elements, and projection mapping, where real photographic textures were applied onto simple CG geometry allowing for more complicated camera moves.

Miniatures were also contemplated. "But we were traveling so fast," says Knoll, "that most of the time something that is way on the horizon at the beginning of a shot is then behind the camera by the end—which would have meant impractically large miniatures. Where we had closed environments like the canyons, we could do them in miniature, but that wasn't very often."

Eventually, Knoll turned to the relatively new area of projection mapping. "We had actually first done projection mapping on *Terminator 2*," he explains, "which is the idea of taking a photographed image, projecting it onto geometry, and then moving the geometry around. We'd also used this on *Hook*, where we took a 2D matte painting, built CG geometry that matched the painting, and then projected the painting onto that to make what amounts to an image warp that was perspective correct in 3D. It took that 2D matte painting edge off it and kept it moving." The technique was more fully explored on *Mission: Impossible*, *Star Trek: First Contact*, and the *Star Wars* Special Editions. "I had been talking to a friend at Electric Image," recalls Knoll, "and I explained this idea of camera mapping and it took a little while to explain what I wanted to do. And he suddenly saw it, 'Oh the UV co-ordinates come from a projection into a camera frustum. Oh I can write that in like an hour!' And he wrote me a little plugin for Electric Image where you could pass it a camera and the geometry you wanted to texture from it, and it was really easy to use." Knoll believed he could apply these projection-mapping

techniques to the podrace environments by drawing on the miniatures expertise of ILM's Model Shop. "We thought we could take a photograph of a miniature and do this image-warping trick with it," states Knoll. "Paul Huston at ILM did a test with one of the mushroom-shaped rocks. He built a model of it 18-inches high, just out of foam and plaster, then painted it all up with nice textures and it looked like it could go in a movie. He took it out into the parking lot and took some really nice detailed photographs of it."

"Then he used a MicroScibe Digitizer, which had encoders on the rotating axes," adds Knoll. "The device would read out the coordinates in 3D space of the probe on the end of the arm, and you could collect a whole bunch of points on the surface and then triangulate the points into a polygonal mesh. He would take that model and do a low-res decimation of it, so he had a crude CG model that was the basic shape of the original model."

That's when the projection-mapping tool was employed—to project photographs of the mushroom back onto the matching CG geometry. "That was pretty magical because when you looked at it, it looked liked a photograph, because it was a photograph," states Knoll. "You could move around it in perspective like you had just done a motion-control move on it. It's an amazing and powerful technique—now we could make many duplicates of these models. And we could mix and match fully rendered things with projection-mapped things and build up to almost arbitrary complexity."

Pirates of the Caribbean: The Curse of the Black Pearl

Audiences watching Gore Verbinski's *Pirates of the Caribbean: The Curse of the Black Pearl* (2003) were treated to a major surprise when it was revealed that Captain Barbossa (Geoffrey Rush) and his ship's crew turn into skeletal beings under moonlight. As visual effects supervisor for ILM on the film, Knoll oversaw the creation of the pirate skeletons as digital characters, as well as their human-to-skeleton transformations as they pass through shafts of moonlight.

For the fully digital characters—first revealed on the ship the Black Pearl—production filmed actors carrying out actions such as hoisting sails and scrubbing the decks. These performances would later be replicated on a motion-capture stage, with the mocap data used to drive the CG skeletons together with keyframe animation. Plates of the empty ship had also been filmed so that ILM could insert their digital characters into the scenes. This was particularly challenging if the skeletons had to interact with a real actor. "We'd typically shoot a reference pass with the actor to be replaced with a CG skeleton," explains Knoll, "and then the actor would move out and we'd shoot our humans talking to an empty space in the plate. Then we'd put our CG character in—in some cases keyframe or motion

captured—along with complicated cloth sims for their ragged clothing."

The transition shots, however, involved another layer of subtle visual-effects work. "In these shots, somebody started off as live action and then turned into the skeleton," describes Knoll. "The only technique that really made any sense for that was shooting the actor in their picture costume, as though they were on both sides of the shot, and then machinating it carefully, rendering the CG skeleton, and compositing a transition in the shot. The tricky part was that obviously the skeletons are going to be a little narrower than the real actor, so the backgrounds needed some clean-up. So we'd shoot clean plates, mostly as an aid for the folks doing the paint-outs."

Despite the labor-intensive effects work, Knoll says that the technique had several advantages. "While the paint-out was a bit of a pain, the crew got better and better at doing it. It meant that some of the things that had traditionally been very difficult in the past—having to shoot a reference pass and an empty plate pass and then editors having to maintain a reference cut and an empty plate cut with the shot lengths not always the same, which then made for sound problems—were no

[1] Geoffrey Rush as Captain Barbossa begins the transformation into his skeletal form as he enters the moonlight.

[2] Artists at ILM blended Geoffrey Rush's live-action performance with his digital skeleton counterpart.

[1]

[2]

[3] The digital, skeletal Barbossa followed Rush's live-action performance.

longer a problem. And then previously the performances weren't always as good because the actors were pantomiming to nothing, so they didn't quite know where to look. And the camera operator was framing a little off because they were framing more generically."

"Well," concludes Knoll, "all of that went away when we were just using the plate that the actor was in. The performances were better, eye-lines were perfect, there was no need for a parallel edit—we got better results when they were right there in the frame." The direct result was a more convincing transition and final performance,

plus a new methodology that Knoll would take into the next *Pirates of the Caribbean* film, *Dead Man's Chest*, for the character of Davy Jones.

Pirates of the Caribbean: Dead Man's Chest

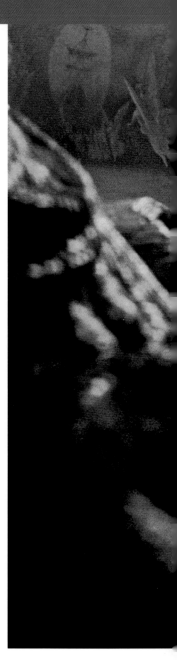

Knoll's experience with the skeleton pirates on *The Curse of the Black Pearl* led straight to the creation of the memorable Davy Jones (Bill Nighy)—a cursed human who had now become part octopus, part lobster, and part man—in *Dead Man's Chest* (2006). "Those shots where we had to exactly copy the actor's performance on the *Black Pearl* were massively painstaking," admits Knoll, "and a lot of manual effort went into matchmoving those, because we didn't have any good references to where all the joint positions were—the characters were wearing big overcoats and layers of wardrobe."

"When Davy Jones came up," says Knoll, "and we knew that the actor had to absolutely be on set, we had to figure out how to get the best motion reference that we could. Since he was going to be replaced, you'd never see him in costume and that meant we could have him dressed in anything we wanted."

Knoll wanted to acquire something equivalent or close to motion capture data on set. "We thought, what if we had our picture camera and we had a couple of high-definition video cameras at cross angles, could we use that to try and triangulate the positions of the joints and get the poor man's equivalent of motion capture on set? We asked our R&D department if they could come up with something that was lightweight, had a small on-set footprint, was robust, and had no shooting constraints."

The result was iMocap, which allowed Nighy to wear a special gray suit with markers on it that would be tracked with specially written software utilizing the video feeds from the on-set cameras. Says Knoll: "It gave us the quality of data you'd get on a motion-capture stage and it was something we could do wherever we were— on a stage or in the pouring rain. It really allowed us to transfer the skeletal performance onto a CG character."

iMocap helped animators handle the body motions for Jones and members of his crew, while the facial animation was implemented manually. "We decided that iMocap was a big enough piece of technology to bite off and dedicate a whole show to," notes Knoll. "So the facial animation involved painstaking attention to detail by the artist to dial in shapes until we thought we could faithfully reproduce Bill's performance, especially the eyes. Since then we've continued to develop all those tools and extended it to facial mocap."

Acquiring the performance via iMocap was perhaps half of bringing Davy Jones to life—the remainder lay in simulating his characteristic tentacles and rendering them with absolute photorealism. "The tentacles were all being driven by a chain of segmented rigid bodies," explains Knoll. "Imagine a tentacle cut up into little slices that are all rigid bodies, with motorized joints between those bodies so you can animate the angles between them. Then we had a control system that had seven or eight parameters, like curling radius and speed, and ratio of tip to base, to control the behaviors."

"We also added this stickiness idea," says Knoll. "Rigid bodies don't really have a notion of static friction or stickiness. So the analogy was, imagine a piece of wet spaghetti against a leather jacket. It's not just going to slide, it's going to stick and then you can peel it off."

The surface quality of Davy Jones' skin had to be similar to an octopus—translucent, scattery, and with a moist quality. For that, ILM employed a rendering technique called "sub-surface scattering" that emulated the way light scatters as it enters the skin. "I wanted him to look a bit like there couldn't just be a guy in makeup playing him," says Knoll. "We were doing the look development on it and I kept saying push the sub-surface scattering. More! And everybody thought I was crazy. I'd say, 'No, double! Two or three times that!' They thought I was insane. They thought it would look like a gummy bear. It's pretty crazy when you look at it—Davy is nothing but scatter—there's no diffuse in him at all."

[1] The CG character's tentacles were one of the many attributes that could be "directed" by ILM artists. "If you wanted Davy to start off normal and get angry and agitated during a shot," explains Knoll, "you could dial up the speed and the curling strength, and he would suddenly look like he was getting angrier as the shot went along."

Pacific Rim

Giant 25-story tall robot Jaegers battling equally giant Kaiju monsters. That was the challenge set by director Guillermo del Toro for *Pacific Rim* (2013), tasking Knoll and ILM to craft fully digital characters often fighting in water or among city streets. Despite the fantastical nature of the film, Knoll immediately looked for a scientific solution to selling the scale and ferocity of the Jaeger/Kaiju encounters. "I come from a whole family of scientists and engineers," says Knoll, "so my first thought was, 'What are the physics of these things fighting and how can that inform us about what this can look like?'"

[1] For the look of the giant Kaiju, ILM referenced crabs, gorillas, reptiles, bats, and dinosaurs. Along with the CG creatures, ILM also had to craft the ocean and pouring rain with fluid simulations during the battles.

[1]

[2] The Jaeger robot Gipsy Danger walks the streets of Hong Kong on the lookout for a Kaiju.

Knoll knew that artistically the biggest challenge was going to be depicting the fights as if they could be filmed for real, with the right speed versus the right scale. Normally, such enormous bodies would be shown moving slower to represent accurate physics, but del Toro did not want the robots or creatures to feel lumbering. "If we were actually shooting these robots as guys in a suit," explains Knoll, "you'd have to film that at 150 plus frames per second for the gravity to feel right. This would mean slowing things down by a factor of six or so, and Guillermo felt that was going to be too slow."

"One of the big aesthetic challenges was trying to find the right speed for things, however, we didn't want it to feel like we'd undermined the scale too much either," adds Knoll. "And how that was going to interact with water and building destruction simulations was another thing. My big fear was that if we cheated the speed of the characters, that might look fine by itself, but the characters are never in isolation. They're often in water, and the fluid simulation would blow up if you moved them too fast. Or, if you're in a city where you're knocking over buildings, your rigid-body sims won't look realistic."

The Jaegers would also be shown in states of readiness and repair inside massive hangars. To enable the filmmakers to stage shots that would feature both the large robots and the much smaller humans, Knoll enlisted the help of an augmented reality tool on a tablet with pre-rendered wide hangar virtual environments that could illustrate what the final location would look like once visual effects were complete.

"The other big aesthetic thing we had to consider," says Knoll, "was that Guillermo wanted to do this wild palette and he had all this concept art he had done with really bright saturated colors. He kept describing them as operatic and theatrical—they were beautiful. I was used to more muted palettes, so trying to embrace that broad color spectrum, but still trying to make it believable was really challenging."

9 > Robert Legato

From epic historical dramas to scorching thrillers, Robert Legato's experience as a visual effects supervisor spans numerous productions. His film credits include *Interview with the Vampire, Apollo 13, Titanic, What Lies Beneath, Harry Potter and the Sorcerer's Stone, Bad Boys II, The Aviator, The Departed, Shine a Light, Avatar, Hugo,* and *The Wolf of Wall Street.* Legato was awarded an Academy Award for achievement in visual effects for his work on *Titanic* and *Hugo,* and was nominated for *Apollo 13.*

Legato considers early contributions to the television series *Star Trek: The Next Generation* and *Deep Space Nine* (for both of which he received Primetime Emmys) as a training ground for his current approach to visual effects—getting things done in a short period of time, prioritizing, and doing more quality work with less.

"Because *Star Trek* was a TV show and you didn't have much time to explore things in advance, you'd just try different approaches from week to week," he says. "I also considered only designing my shots to emulate feature film shots—all of which were shot on film, incidentally—rather than limiting my own vision by only designing for television's smaller scope and budget."

With so many visual effects to complete for each *Star Trek* show, Legato soon found that he was gaining wide experience of the entire filmmaking process and would use that to help design shots. "I learned very quickly that if you only designed a wide shot, you limited what could be done to enhance the visuals with sound effects for example. But if you decided to break it down into two or more shots, and could get in really close to some moving parts or some macro action, then the SFX designers had much more to work with. The added sound created a much bigger feature film experience. I also explored very graphic lighting and more interesting and sophisticated camera choreography from week to week. I became much more of a 'sequence' director and supervisor, rather than just a shot-driven one. Having several pieces of film edited together—illustrating a moment, rather than that one shot—created a more interesting filmic experience and powerful storytelling opportunities."

"Because I'm also an editor, I could design, shoot, and then edit to maximize the effect I was going for,"

adds Legato. "I'd be able to alter or improve the idea after the fact to make it work much better. I always thought there was something more interesting I could add later, rather than having to solve all of the problems on the stage. Consequently, every shot or sequence was a work in progress, and that was a philosophy that I took to movies."

Star Trek was also Legato's first exposure to digital compositing and helped him break into the visual effects studio Digital Domain. Here he would combine his on-set practical and miniatures expertise with the digital knowledge and directly apply that to films such as *Interview with the Vampire, Apollo 13,* and *Titanic.* Still, according to Legato, many visual effects challenges remain photographic in nature, such as his experience in shooting and lighting the miniature underwater submersible scenes for *Titanic.*

"I was struggling to get the right look," says Legato, "and cinematographer Caleb Deschanel—who was originally going to work on the film—said something strange to me at the time, which was, 'Why don't you just backlight the ship?' As the Titanic was so deep, the only logical light source would have to come from the on-board lighting from the Mir subs. I just thought it was crazy to consider lighting from anything besides the real on-board Mir lights. But, because he is such a genius cinematographer I thought I better consider his idea carefully. I took blue Kino Flos—large fluorescent studio lights—and literally hung them up above the wreck and set the exposure at the very lowest level for just the blue layer of film to see. The level was so low, way below exposure, I would have to take the little sphere off the lightmeter just to be able to read it. I set the exposure,

[1] Robert Legato.

[2] For **Titanic**, Legato would pioneer both large-scale miniature effects, digital imagery, and compositing to bring James Cameron's film to life.

all backlit, and made it about five-stops underexposed, so it basically could only add to the Mir miniature flashlight bulbs as the light falls off in the distance. The pre-flashed blue layer had now just enough exposure to become visible, while the untreated red and green layer would remain jet black. It created this very natural phenomenon where in deep water the light naturally attenuates from warm—close to the light itself—to deep blue in the distance, just like Jim's real-life photography of the wreck. It became an identical photographic mate to the real footage and they were easily intercut without any tell-tale sign to clue the audience that they were actually watching a miniature."

However, for Legato, making shots look real is typically only half the battle. The audience also has to be emotionally connected to what is on the screen. "I think a lot of the problem with CG effects work today, even if it's amazing work, is that you know it's not real," says Legato. "You know there's not a million people

in an army so you're really not wrapped up in the same emotion as if it were real—the suspension of disbelief is shattered through no fault of the artist. The largess of a shot that can only be staged with CG creates a wall of difference from our epic films of yesteryear. We knew those were all real people or places and were staggered by the sheer production value of a David Lean film."

"There might only be a handful of truly epic shots due to practicality, but the rest of the sequence cinematically sets up the crescendo of these moments," continues Legato. "Now, all the shots are crescendo moments, with little cinematic setup to build to a climax. More actually becomes less. One thing I've found with all the films I've worked on is that once you really believe it could have been actually filmed live, then you become much more emotionally wrapped up in what you're looking at. You no longer think it's fake, or miniatures, or computer generated."

Apollo 13

Footage of rocket launches to the moon captivated the public in the 1960s and 1970s. When Ron Howard sought to re-create the launch and journey of the ill-fated Apollo 13 mission in his 1995 movie of the same name, he tapped Legato and Digital Domain for the task. But the visual effects supervisor was adamant that the shots were not just built from the famous stock launch footage. "As a movie viewer," says Legato, "every time I see a piece of stock footage I get taken out of the movie. I feel like it is not the film I was watching. And that's something I wouldn't want to do."

That meant that everything from the launch-pad sequence to the space environments and splashdown would be realized with visual effects—ultimately a combination of miniatures, CG animation elements, and practical photography. "I wanted to re-create those moments as practically as possible. It's pretty simple stuff when you break it down. The gas that is shooting out of the engines could be fire extinguishers, the ice coming down onto the rocket could be wax, and the capsule landing in the ocean could be thrown out of a helicopter and land in the real ocean water."

The move away from stock footage also came from Legato's desire to present a new way of viewing these famous moments. "I wanted it to remind you of a shot you've seen before, but not seen quite that way," he says. "So it has a sense of familiarity, but you've never actually experienced it like that before. Anything we've seen before has all been shot with long lenses because the cameras had to be pretty safely away from the launch area. To put you more into the film experience I created similar looking angles and compositions, but with very short lenses. There is a different emotional quality that you get with a long lens, which is more voyeuristic and distant; a short lens gives you immediacy—it feels like you're right there."

"Also," says Legato, "I think our memories are totally infused with our emotions. As an experiment I tried to find the most evocative and iconic shots from the real stock footage and asked a roomful of people to describe them back to me. Sure enough, they described them back, but filled them with their own sense of awe. I

discovered they embellished what they saw because they were excited about the material and the subject matter—it conjured up romantic memories of the time, even though they saw the material moments ago. The trick became not to film what really happened, but to film what you remember; film the embellished romantic images rather than documentary-looking footage. So that's what I did."

"I learned fairly early on in my career you must trust your instincts," adds Legato. "In this business you have no choice but to trust yourself, because it may be six or seven months before you actually see your idea come to fruition. You have to rely on your initial instinct and not continually question its validity. People along the way will question your instincts and try to steer you away from them due to their own limitations and comfort level in playing it safe."

During production of the launch shots, Legato specifically listened to heroic music in the screening room while reviewing shots. "It was meant to be an heroic, soaring moment," he says, "so I'd play music during dailies and then go back and alter the shot based on whatever musical inspiration moved me. It had to do with what felt right, rather than what—intellectually—was right."

Legato also pushed the filmmakers to ensure that the visual effects shots of the rocket and capsule matched the feel of the rest of the film. "They originally wanted me to shoot all the exterior ship shots first, without seeing how the live-action scene played out," he relates. "They said, 'Why can't you do that in advance, they don't seem related?' Well, my response was, 'Because I don't know what the movie is yet.' I knew from my *Star Trek* days that it was really hard to incorporate the exterior shots in an emotional way if I didn't see the scenes surrounding it. So when I saw how Ron Howard had shot the footage inside the capsule and the type of emotion he was achieving, it changed or altered the way the exteriors should be captured. If the characters felt isolated, then our shots had to fit that. If it was an action shot, then that would change the approach too."

[1] A Saturn V rocket launches from Kennedy Space Center in this shot completed by Digital Domain.

[2] Separation of the first stage of the Saturn V rocket carrying the Apollo 13 crew—an effect that appears to be photographed from inside the rocket's second-stage cylinder.

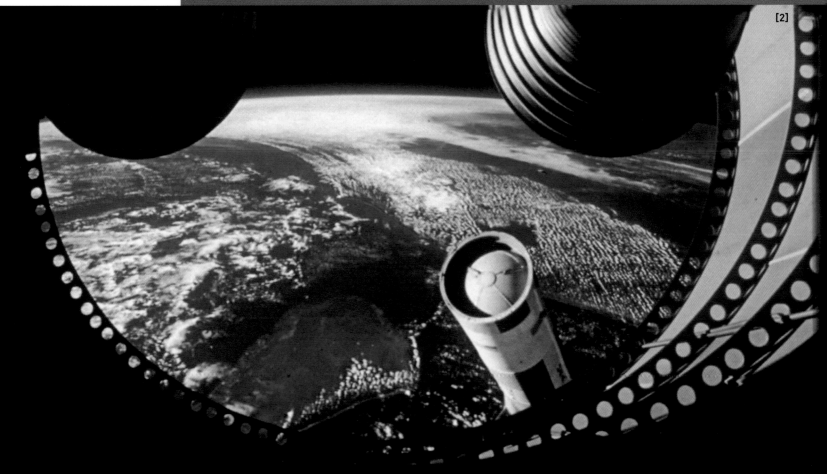

[2]

Titanic

James Cameron's *Titanic* (1997) presented Legato with a multitude of effects challenges—there were sweeping aerial shots of the doomed ocean liner, dramatic scenes of the ship and its passengers sinking, underwater views of the ship in its final resting place, and transitions between 1912 and the present day.

For the "ship at sea" shots, Legato's approach was to make it feel as if it had been filmed for real, even though the ship was a 45-foot model shot with motion control cameras, integrated into CG water, and populated with motion captured CG sailors and passengers. "To get that realistic feeling," say Legato, "I would photograph it like you're doing a modern cruise commercial. That's something you'd use a helicopter to photograph, so I would confine the shots to what a helicopter could do. I went out in a helicopter and shot a ship at sea and did some moves as reference, and then emulated those moves and restrictions for the motion-control shots. The only time you've seen a shot like that was in a film that was filmed practically and you tend to believe things filmed practically more often than not."

At that time, CG water was still a very difficult proposition, but Legato insisted that a digital ocean was necessary so he could move the camera and create the transition shots that melted from one period to another. "We looked to a company called Arete, which was essentially creating water sims for the military," recalls Legato. "From satellites they could view a ship's wake and because of the nature of the wake and how it was formed they could determine what ship it was. I saw a picture of it and thought it was remarkably good, although the art was not there because they were scientists using sim technology for a non-artistic purpose. But I thought if we took their base technology and added artistic controls we could in essence motion control realistic-looking water. We could create any camera move we wanted and have a perfect water plate created for it."

Legato says the decision to do CG water was actually a controversial choice at the time. "People thought it could not be done," he says. "And I thought, 'Well, then it's now worth doing!' I didn't know exactly how I could

do it, I just knew that it could be done. All I had to do was get enough geniuses in a room and every time they hit a stumbling block I'd encourage them to go further and further. We literally cracked the code to do it. That's the interesting thing about this business—you start with the art portion of it, and then you have the technology created to make the art happen. The whole idea of CG water in particular was to create the transition shots to melt from one place to another. That was the cornerstone of the movie for me."

Similarly, motion-captured actors had not been popularly featured in many films at that point, but Legato felt that approach would offer him flexibility in performance and positioning. "No one had really ever used mocap to capture a person on film—it was more for a skeleton, or a knight's armor, or a robot. We had to melt from one state of the Titanic to the other, so

[1] Scenes of the Titanic upended in the ocean after hitting an iceberg included practical stunts filmed on a tilting platform.

[2] This final shot features a miniature ship, live-action actors, motion-captured actors, and digital water and stack smoke, all composited by Digital Domain.

I needed to be able to control the people on the ship. I had to do repeat passes and forced motion capture into the forefront of that. So then it became worth doing. And we had a film worth doing it on."

Just as challenging were the underwater scenes of the Titanic wreck, as Legato's visual effects shots of miniature subs and parts of the ship had to intercut seamlessly with actual footage acquired by Cameron at the site. To do this, Legato's team built a miniature wreck and subs and filmed them inverted—for greater control—on a smoke stage.

"It was very emotional watching the original wreck footage that Jim Cameron personally shot," acknowledges Legato. "It was very moving, and beautifully haunting. One of our prouder moments was when we realized that the audience could not tell the difference between the real wreck and our fabricated

footage. They were as emotionally moved by our miniature 18-foot wreck model shot in smoke with Mir subs the size of small footballs as they were by the real thing."

The Aviator

In *The Aviator* (2004)—Martin Scorsese's biographical account of famed filmmaker and aviation pioneer, Howard Hughes—Legato had to make the most of what he describes as a relatively low visual effects budget to produce complicated flying sequences, recreate vintage aircraft, and deliver at least one dramatic crash. The final VFX shots involved miniatures, forced-perspective models, remote-control scaled plane replicas, and computer-generated aircraft and environments.

"It was an interesting film because some of the limitations led me to what the film became," says Legato. "Because it's a film about that time period and that particular filmmaker, I decided we would use as many practical effects as we could. For example, we enjoyed building very exacting replicas of Hughes' planes, which actually flew exactly as the originals did (albeit in miniature), design flaws and all.

They were photographed with a helicopter as if they were full size. I thought if we could do it for real, why not? And then when you're forced into shooting it for real you're also forced into the realities of the physicality

of live-action photography. It automatically creates verisimilitude and helps blur the line between illusion and reality."

Legato took the same approach for scenes of Hughes (Leonardo DiCaprio) crashing an XF-11 reconnaissance aircraft into houses in Beverly Hills. To realize the entire crash as economically as possible, Legato's team set about previsualizing the entire sequence, not just the visual effects shots. "We used the previs system to preview the crash scene, cutting it together and creating an editorial rhythm with shots I could only film live, which amounted to a locked-off camera and an exterior model. We'd also lived with what would have naturally created the same dynamics in the actual crash, without trying to embellish them with artificial camera moves or angles. Whatever happened in real life happened in our recreation."

"There was no way our budget limitations would allow us to create a big-budget action-film sequence," notes Legato. "This more or less forced our point of view to witness the crash as Hughes did. That proved to be

[1] The aftermath of the XF-11 crash. To film the crash, a 1/4-scale model was constructed of the three houses Hughes plows into. A miniature plane was then mounted on a track and rigged to push through the model buildings.

best for the film and made that particular sequence different from all the others. It was very nicely reviewed and not only was it inexpensive to produce, but it also created a unique Scorsese-styled sequence."

That previs methodology involved a virtual camera approach. The previs shots could be controlled via typical camera movements in real time, providing Legato and other filmmakers with immediate feedback and angles that would reflect what could be captured on set. "That actually came out of working with Michael Bay on *Bad Boys II*," says Legato. "He had a bunch of previs artists and he got a little frustrated that he could never quite get the shot he envisaged because he couldn't describe it well enough to an artist who had never picked up an actual camera in real life—he just wanted to pick up a camera and show them what a 14mm lens looked like a few inches off the ground etc. I helped them with the previs of that, and I became frustrated too. I would grab the mouse, but the mouse is not the same as a camera—it doesn't let you provide these visceral experiences and let you try being higher or lower with real-time feedback—you usually do these adjustments very fast in live action, but you really don't do that with a computer because you don't have real-time feedback. I liken it to trying to compose music at a piano one note at a time, with each note separated by several minutes."

"So on *The Aviator*," continues Legato, "where I had to recreate his pivotal XF-11 crash, which is a scene I'd never really done before, I needed very practical experience photographing these shots. My gut feeling

was for getting it in the same way a live-action cameraman would do it. And that also dovetailed right into editing as well. You really want full dailies describing the whole action from many different angles to edit with, and you don't want just the one four-second shot that someone on a computer made for you."

"So the virtual camera came out of the frustration of my artistic expression being limited to existing tools that really didn't reflect the type of work I do. Why not make a tool that mimics a real live set or experience? With a virtual camera I can walk around a mocap stage and frame up instantly any angle I choose on any dolly, crane, or hand-held camera and shoot the scene from that angle beginning to end. I can change angles just like in live action and shoot it again, and again. Now I have a full set of dailies from which to decide what angle works best, double and triple cut for effect and have the freedom to reshoot as often as I wish. It became a very organic way of working, which mimics how live action has been shot and edited since the beginning of film."

Interestingly, Legato demonstrated an adaption of the system with motion capture to James Cameron, who immediately recognized its potential in helping to make his ambitious film *Avatar*. "The system meant you had everything in front of you to preview your movie shot for shot," says Legato, "and you could get a real editorial rhythm because it starts to feel like real life, and not a typical stiff cartoon-looking previs. What this demonstrates is that it is always the art you want to create that forces you to come up with technology to realize it."

Hugo

Among the adventures in Martin Scorsese's *Hugo* (2011) is a celebration of the life of Georges Méliès, a man often considered the father of the visual-effects industry for his innovative experiments in multiple exposure, time-lapse photography, and hand-painted color filmmaking. Legato freely admits that he was not aware of most of Méliès' contributions to the art of effects before starting on *Hugo* besides the iconic imagery associated with the filmmaker's 1902 film *A Trip to the Moon*.

"But the great thing about movies is that it causes you to study," reflects Legato. "So when I started studying Méliès' complete works it was like, 'Holy shit, this guy is some kind of stone-cold genius!' This artist should be rediscovered much like how the story rediscovers him. He is literally the father of what we do. And before this film I disappointingly short shrifted him and his huge impact on the industry by my own lack of research on his life and works. In the end I became an enormous fan of that exciting pioneering time period and the incredible

ingenuity it spawned. He was really the first visual effects supervisor, inventing techniques to realize the art and innovation his crazy concepts demanded. The ideas were just wild and he found a way to express them on film. He first created the art and then invented the technology to realize them on film—a true master of the medium."

"One story from the film," describes Legato, "was when we totally recreated Méliès' glasshouse studio where he used to make all his movies, with everyone now in period costumes, and genuine props shot against exact replicas of his sets. We found ourselves incredibly moved realizing the only other people to ever witness this exact image in person were Méliès himself and his crew. As soon as you walk in there you have goosebumps because you realize you are on very sacred ground."

Hugo, which follows the story of a young boy living in the French railway station of Gare Montparnasse, included extensive visual effects work that Legato

[1]

[1] Hugo Cabret (Asa Butterfield) evades capture outside the Gare Montparnasse train station.

sought to base on both techniques and imagery from the era. That meant the use of miniatures and practical effects were combined with the latest techniques in 3D and state-of-the-art stereo. "Some shots required the very same age-old techniques that Méliès used to great effect," says Legato. "We did our very best to create a loving homage to the signature scenes created by Méliès and other pioneers such as the Lumière brothers."

"We thought 'let's try and recreate for a modern audience the same sensation Méliès' audience would have felt for the first time'—that was the guiding light to making the movie," adds Legato. "We used the latest 3D stereo techniques to help our experienced audience get to see some of these illusions in a new and surprising way. As early as 1916, the Lumière Brothers were experimenting with 3D and had Méliès continued making films he would have used this remarkable technology with his own unique vision. The whole thing just became such a labor of love and one of the greatest experiences I'll ever have. To have the opportunity to do Georges Méliès justice and then be crazily rewarded for it alongside some of the finest craftsmen in the business, led by a legendary director and eminent film historian, well, that's what dreams are made of."

"I have the greatest respect for the pioneers who created the foundation of our careers today," says Legato. "Completely fearless to go down a path never traveled to further the art form we now enjoy. They were all so incredibly smart and brave. My own career has been defined by keeping that same spirit alive. Don't be afraid of doing something that hasn't been done before—instead be exhilarated and motivated by the challenge. You can't possibly succeed if you're too afraid to fail."

[2] Robert Legato (far left) on the set of **Hugo**.

10 > Joe Letteri

Gollum from *The Lord of the Rings*, the Na'vi in *Avatar*, Caesar from the new *Planet of the Apes* films—these are all characters that senior visual effects supervisor and Weta Digital director Joe Letteri has helped create. He has fostered a continuously innovative approach at the New Zealand-based studio, winning four visual effects Oscars (for *The Two Towers*, *The Return of the King*, *King Kong*, and *Avatar*), and picking up five further nominations in the process.

Letteri began his career working in computer graphics at Industrial Light & Magic in the early 1990s. "I started off doing computer graphics partly because I was interested in it," says Letteri. "I had an interest in natural phenomenon. The science of fractals was new at the time and those were things that were kind of intriguing in that you could use computers to understand the natural world and how to portray it.

The first film that I worked on was *Star Trek VI: The Undiscovered Country* and the Praxis moon explosion. There was some thinking at the time to try and do that practically, but it was hard to get fire like that at the scale necessary to give it that otherworldly look. Because I'd been experimenting with fractals I'd come up with a way we could do that and get it to work as a 'traveling through space in a wind of fire look.' The film gave me a great canvas to work with."

Letteri then contributed to the visual effects of *Jurassic Park*. "We had to go to the microscopic level and ask what makes skin look real?" he recalls of the time. "A lot of these principles you actually see everywhere in the world once you start to look for them. We had to look at the real world, then pull the science together to actually render it, and then learn about filmmaking at the same time. Things like, why does a cinematographer put the lights where they do, what's important about the composition of the shot, and how does movement convey reality and suspense and drama? It was a real crash course in filmmaking, as well as developing the tools we needed to create the images."

When Letteri moved to Wellington, New Zealand, to supervise the visual effects on *The Two Towers*, he continued that analysis of the real world in his work.

"I started off with just an examination of natural phenomena, but it's lead into this ongoing exploration of what do we see in the natural world, and why do we react to certain things in the way that we do? How do you take those moments—as a filmmaker does—and build them into a narrative that audiences will want to follow through? It's been a unique environment of crafting things that aren't really real, but we want to make them look real and we want them to feel like they're something we want to experience."

"To do that," says Letteri, "you have to get under the hood and figure out why things look the way they do—why eyes look the way they do and why when you're talking to someone, subtle motions of the eyes can speak volumes about what that character is thinking. And also how does an editor take that and use it to get the audience to understand the story arc."

With a wealth of film and effects experience behind him, Letteri has also learned a great deal and is passionate about advancing the technology, while maintaining the artistry. "I'm always thinking about how to craft an illusion that is going to be interesting and make an audience want to sit up and take notice. You go from very detailed explanations—sometimes heavily science-based—to thinking, 'Now where does the artistry come in, and how do you use these tools to create story and how does this fit into the overall flow of making the film?' Film is a very collaborative medium and you have all these influences coming together. I was very lucky to come into this business at a time when there were opportunities for new ideas and new stories to be told. You're always looking for that convergence of the two to allow you to move the art forward."

[1] Joe Letteri (center) on the set of **Dawn of the Planet of the Apes**. With him are director Matt Reeves (right) and production designer James Chinlund (left).

[2]

[2] The apes storm the Golden Gate Bridge in **Rise of the Planet of the Apes**.

The Lord of the Rings: The Two Towers and The Return of the King

When Letteri came to Weta Digital, his first challenge was helping to complete the enormous visual effects requirements for the remaining two films in Peter Jackson's *The Lord of the Rings* trilogy. In particular, the visual effects supervisor tackled Gollum, a troubled creature who once owned the One Ring. In both *The Two Towers* (2002) and *The Return of the King* (2003), Gollum would appear on screen as a completely CG—and central—character, performed on set and via motion capture by actor Andy Serkis and then brought to life by the artists at Weta Digital under Letteri's supervision.

"One of the things that I learned from doing *Jurassic Park* is that performance is important. So is realism, obviously, but dinosaurs are big scary creatures," says Letteri, discussing how he approached Gollum. "When it was time to look at human-like characters, we realized there were other subtleties going on. Rather than just create creatures to mostly scare you, I was intrigued

about creating performances that you engaged with. And Gollum had that—he needed to be part of the story, and the film required him to be interacting directly with other actors. He had to not only appear absolutely real, but hold your attention and be engaging."

Letteri credits Serkis with infusing Gollum with the requisite split personality—representing his former self, the hobbit Sméagol, and the creature he had become. "We were really lucky to be working with Andy Serkis," says Letteri. "He took on that role in such an intuitive way. He took on Gollum and worked in the scene with the other actors and he gave us the blueprint for the character that we could follow."

On set, Serkis wore a one-color suit and would perform the scene with the actors directly. Additional plates without Serkis, but just the live-action actors, as well as clean background plates, were also captured. Letteri says Jackson was so impressed with Serkis'

[1] Gollum converses with his own reflection in **The Return of the King**.

[1]

[2] Gollum finds himself on a journey with Frodo Baggins (Elijah Wood) and Samwise Gamgee (Sean Astin) in **The Return of the King**.

on-set performance that he wanted to capture his physical actions more accurately so that they could be translated into the CG character. "We thought, 'Gee, if we can just capture his actions directly maybe we could use it—and motion capture in those days was still a pretty new technology—it was still a 'science' thing. But we set about transforming it into a real production setup. We turned the motion capture stage into a real stage with all the same protocols and working methodologies you have in a real stage—Peter could direct Andy just like any other actor, but using motion capture cameras instead of motion picture cameras."

That meant that Weta Digital had the means to use Serkis' movements as an anatomical guide in animating Gollum. Interestingly, placing him into the shots was originally envisaged as a relatively easy process that involved adding the character to the plates of just live-action actors or empty scenes. But Serkis had given such a great performance that oftentimes the effects

artists used the plates with him in, then rotoscoped him out and inserted the digital character. Letteri and Weta Digital also pushed forward the technology behind rendering Gollum's skin. "With human-like skin we needed to understand more how that behaves," explains Letteri. "It's the translucency, the way light permeates through the skin and scatters around and gives you the richness of color. That phenomenon is called sub-surface scattering. Being able to develop that was one of the cornerstones of being able to develop the human-like skin that we needed for Gollum."

"The combination of that detailed performance from Andy and figuring out how to make skin look really realistic—plus all the other aspects we had learned in visual effects up until then—meant we were really able to put Gollum in there and make him part of the story."

The Hobbit: An Unexpected Journey

Serkis would return to perform Gollum in Jackson's *The Hobbit: An Unexpected Journey* (2012), the first of three *Hobbit* films based on Tolkien's novel. Weta Digital had continued developing several motion capture, animation, and rendering technologies as a direct result of its experiences on *The Lord of the Rings* films. Letteri saw the new Hobbit films as a chance to capitalize on these new tools and approaches to produce even more believable performances.

"When we were working with Andy on the original Rings trilogy," says Letteri, "there were a lot of things working so well on the body we thought, 'I wonder if we can capture his face?' And if we could really figure out the way this lighting is working on the skin, I wonder if we can do it on a global sense? And if we really like what Andy's doing on the stage, can we capture it all on set instead?"

"When we captured Gollum originally," continues Letteri, "we used motion capture for his body some percentage of the time (still with a ton of keyframe), but his face was entirely keyframed—there was no way at the time that we could consider capturing his face.

"But because we had the animation understanding from the Gollum we worked out how to put the two ideas together and do facial capture, which we also took to *King Kong* and then *Avatar*, where Jim Cameron wanted to break free of the mocap stage and make the whole world a virtual production stage. So he brought the idea of mounting the head rig on the actor's faces so they had freedom of movement, and this idea of a virtual camera so he could actually see the performances unfolding in this virtual world."

Further development took place when Serkis was enlisted as Caesar in *Rise of the Planet of the Apes*. "Here we thought now wouldn't it be great to figure out how to capture Andy's performance on the day," says Letteri. "We didn't want to ask him to come back and do it again. Whatever he does with James Franco and the other

[1] Motion-capture and animation techniques learned from creating Gollum were applied to other characters in the film, including the three Trolls.

[1]

[2] Gollum returned to the screen, again performed on set by Andy Serkis, but this time with improved motion- and facial-capture techniques.

actors is what goes into the movie. So we came up with a way to make on-stage motion capture work. There can be a lot of interference with motion capture cameras and film cameras and lights, so we had to solve that problem as well."

"So," Letteri notes, "in *The Hobbit* it was kind of like coming back full circle. We thought 'well, now we can do things that we set up doing 12 years earlier.' Andy's 'riddles in the dark' scene with Gollum was the first scene we did. We had Andy on stage capturing it live—it all just worked and it was a great homecoming and a great way to kick off the *Hobbit* trilogy."

King Kong

Jackson's next film, *King Kong* (2005), would see Letteri and Weta Digital amplify their motion capture approach to create the giant gorilla as a fully virtual character. Andy Serkis once again lent his unique on-set mocap experience to the performance, this time going further with facial motion capture and on-set interaction to portray the emotional connection between Kong and Ann Darrow (Naomi Watts).

"We used the same principles we applied when we'd worked with actors creating virtual characters," outlines Letteri. "As much as possible, we like to have the actors who are driving the virtual character performing with the live-action characters. And that's what we did in *King Kong*—any scene Naomi had where she was interacting

with Kong we had Andy there—he was on-set, on a rostrum or scissor lift, or whatever else he had to be on to get the correct eyeline."

Serkis found several ways to "become" the character of Kong. He studied gorilla footage, and visited the animals at London Zoo and in the wild in Rwanda. On set, the actor also wore a special performance suit that adjusted his posture to suit a primate, giving Weta Digital artists further reference.

After principal photography, Serkis would perform Kong scenes on the motion-capture stage. "In those days we had to ask Andy to go back and recreate the performance on the motion-capture stage," says Letteri. "We'd really done a lot in terms of motion capture for

[1] Naomi Watts, who plays Ann Darrow, in a greenscreen-covered Kong hand piece.

[1]

[2] Weta Digital inserted Watts into the hand grip of Kong and created the New York environment around the characters as the giant gorilla climbs the Empire State Building.

[3] King Kong at his home on Skull Island.

Gollum, so we thought, now that we have the body capture developed, let's do facial capture. It's different to capturing the body because capturing skeletal movements is very mechanical—facial movements are a lot less obvious to translate into a performance." Here, Serkis would perform the scenes with tracking dots stuck to his face in addition to a motion-capture suit—these would help re-target facial features to those of Kong.

As they had done with the skin shading for Gollum, Weta Digital researched and developed a new method for achieving digital fur—necessary for the complicated all-over groom Kong would exhibit. The system involved methods to produce more than three million hairs for the character and have it behave appropriately in both the jungle and New York City environments.

"The connection between Kong and Darrow was really important on this film," notes Letteri, "especially because Kong has no dialog. So it was all facial performance, with our visual effects really selling the believability of this character. But interaction was key. The sound guys even built what they called the Konq-a-lizer for Andy to amplify his voice—he did the Kong voice as they performed the scene live. He'd roar and it would shake the stage! You had everything going on to get the drama between the two actors."

Avatar

For *Avatar* (2009), director James Cameron was drawn to Weta Digital's motion capture, character, and environment prowess to complete the film's visual effects. Cameron established a unique shooting system to gather actor performances in motion-capture suits and facial capture setups, with the addition of a virtual camera system that let him view their digital surroundings in real-time. In addition, live-action photography would be captured with Cameron's own 3D stereoscopic system and high-definition digital cameras.

For Letteri, this new virtual production pipeline was a clear highlight of working on the show. "Just taking the idea of motion capture and facial capture, and tracking a virtual camera in the scene and combining them altogether so that Jim could shoot the movie on a virtual stage—that was fantastic. It was just so powerful being able to see through his virtual camera and see the actors as their characters within the environment. It was in a rough form, as it wouldn't be in the film, but there was enough detail to work out the lighting direction and for composition to lay the groundwork for the film."

Letteri and Weta Digital would take Cameron's resulting blueprint of the film and create the CG characters, vehicles, and environments using several newly developed techniques. One of these had actually been designed for *King Kong*—an implementation of the facial action coding system (FACS). FACS is used to define human facial movements based on particular sections of the face. By isolating the parts of the face

[1] Weta Digital crafted an array of creatures to inhabit Pandora, including this thanator stalking Jake Sully (Sam Worthington).

[1]

[2] The incredible close-up views of Weta Digital's CG characters were made possible with the use of new texture painting software called Mari.

that form certain emotions, effects artists can "dial in" realistic performances to computer-generated characters. Weta Digital used its FACS implementation to translate the facial video capture of the avatars to their CG Na'vi counterparts.

As Cameron's aim was to produce a completely photorealistic world in *Avatar*, Weta Digital also added another breakthrough on the production to make the appearance of its CG creatures, characters, vehicles, and greenery as detailed as possible. This came in the form of an advanced 3D-painting system called Mari. Also developed was a more physically-based muscle and skin system called Tissue, designed to give the Na'vi and all the creatures a more realistic framework from which to build the CG models.

To light and render the vast jungles in the film, Weta Digital also developed new technology. "In a lot of examples up until then," says Letteri, "we'd been taking live-action photography and then creating characters and putting them into the scene, so a lot of the look is decided for you. You know where the trees are and where the light's coming from. In the case of *Avatar* we were creating that all from scratch so we needed a system

that would allow us to essentially work without a net. We created a technique called 'spherical harmonic lighting' to do that. We needed to have a lighting system we could create globally and create the sky and the sun and have it filter down through the trees and bounce around and do what it needed to do to give it the richness you expected it to have.

"*Avatar* really was a great film for us," says Letteri. "It was so vast in its scope that it both willed us and forced us to sit back and assess the state of the art as it had been practiced up until that time. We had to go through every aspect of VFX we were doing—which ones were still valid and which ones we could do better, both because we had to and because we had more resources and computer power available to us."

Rise of the Planet of the Apes and Dawn of the Planet of the Apes

With Rupert Wyatt's *Rise of the Planet of the Apes* (2011) and its sequel, Matt Reeves' *Dawn of the Planet of the Apes* (2014), Weta Digital again demonstrated its technical know-how in virtual production and in delivering photorealistic characters. But these films also highlighted the important role Letteri and his entire visual effects crew were now playing as collaborators in the filmmaking process.

"I think *Rise* and *Dawn* really cemented the relationship between visual effects and live-action filmmaking," suggests Letteri. "We were no longer just there taking measurements and trying to work out what we were going to do after the fact. We were there to support the actors who were the apes in their performance. The filmmakers understood the necessity of us being part of that project from the beginning. The performances were something we had to own—we had to make sure from start to finish we understood what the actors were doing, what the characters needed to do, and we handled that transition all the way through."

Part of that new paradigm of visual-effects integration on the *Apes* films came from Letteri pushing for the motion capture of the apes to be done not only on a

stage, but also outdoors, and on-set where the practical photography was taking place. "When you're doing motion capture on set you're bringing a whole new crew to a set that really hasn't changed in a hundred years or so," he says. "Now we are actually having to rig lights and cameras of our own to capture an aspect of the performance. There's a whole new protocol we have to develop with the camera department and grips and electrical and everyone to integrate that all. It really allowed us to just blend into the production."

"There was a time in the history of filmmaking when cameras became lightweight enough and film stocks became lightweight enough that you could start moving from sound stages to location," adds Letteri, "and it felt like we were trying to do that here. We didn't want to be limited by the technology. If the story you need to tell takes you somewhere remote, we can do that. We can create the tools and integrate them with the film production in a way that lets everyone do what they need to do. The director is unencumbered, the actors perform—we can just be in the moment and capture what we can and then use what we know to craft the finished performances."

[1] Caesar (played by Andy Serkis) in **Dawn of the Planet of the Apes**.

[2] On the set of **Dawn of the Planet of the Apes**, with Andy Serkis performing as Caesar in a motion-capture suit outdoors.

[3] The creation of Caesar in **Rise of the Planet of the Apes**—from the performance capture by Andy Serkis, to the CG ape, fur, and final shot.

Tested on *Rise*, the outdoor motion-capture system was fully implemented on *Dawn* to deal with multiple performers, including Andy Serkis as Caesar and Toby Kebbell as Koba, and withstand extreme conditions in dense forests, pouring rain, and extreme heat. "Outside is the worst case," explains Letteri. "The bright sunlight reflecting off chrome automobile bumpers and that sort of thing can really fool motion-capture cameras."

Letteri notes too that having the motion capture volumes on set was extremely helpful for the actors.

"We created this side stage for the actors and here they could do their rehearsals as apes and actually see what their actions would look like on digital models. So then when they walked onto the set they were comfortable that they knew what their performance would be and we were there to support that. It was also a way to critique their performance, meaning you can start having conversations about how the character is going to come across in the final film at that early stage."

11 > **Dennis Muren**

With films like the original *Star Wars* trilogy, *E.T. the Extra-Terrestrial*, *Terminator 2: Judgment Day*, and *Jurassic Park* to his name, Dennis Muren has witnessed both the resurgence of classic visual effects in the late 1970s at Industrial Light & Magic (ILM) and the explosion of digital effects (again at ILM) in the early 1990s. At both junctions he played a critical part in advancing the art and craft of visual effects filmmaking.

Yet Muren—who holds eight Academy Awards for best achievement in visual effects—came close to not being there. "I'd been working in commercials and I was actually ready to get out of the business because there wasn't much work," he says. "But then when *Star Wars* came along I did an interview with John Dykstra and this was my entrance into this crazy group of people who were building mechanics and cameras, and modifying old ones. They were building stuff to get the images that the director wanted, which is totally not the way I had worked before."

Muren worked as a second cameraman on *Star Wars: Episode IV—A New Hope*, as a visual-effects director of photography on *Star Wars: Episode V—The Empire Strikes Back*, and a visual-effects supervisor on *Star Wars: Episode VI—Return of the Jedi*. His impressive resume includes visual-effects supervisory credits on *Dragonslayer*, *E.T. the Extra-Terrestrial*, *Indiana Jones and the Temple of Doom*, *Young Sherlock Holmes*, *Innerspace*, *Empire of the Sun*, *Willow*, *Ghostbusters II*, *The Abyss*, *Terminator 2: Judgment Day*, *Jurassic Park*, *Casper*, *The Lost World: Jurassic Park*, *Star Wars: Episode I—The Phantom Menace*, *A.I. Artificial Intelligence*, *Star Wars: Episode II—Attack of the Clones*, *Hulk*, *War of the Worlds*, and *Super 8*.

Muren's early exposure to film camera effects and optical visual effects was, at first, met with some skepticism. "I was surprised on *Star Wars* that the motion-control stuff was such a great tool, because in some ways it made easy shots more difficult to do" he states. "But you could also do very difficult shots that there was no other way to do at all. It just opened my eyes specifically to how you could design new, amazing shots because you had a new level of control. For me,

this was a way to add an artistic component to a shot, from obscure or overt, with the hope that the viewer would feel the moment as opposed to just viewing it. Since I was a kid, I remember that was always my goal. I wanted to feel the shot emotionally." When digital effects techniques became available, Muren was an early adopter. "I was always saying, 'Well, we really have to just try this and see if it's going to pan out to see if the work is better than with existing techniques. I really just embraced it because my interest has always been on the final image, not on the tools used to make it."

A game-changer project was *Young Sherlock Holmes* (1985), in which ILM would realize one of the first all-digital characters on screen—the stained-glass knight. "We had a computer graphics group and I really was pushing them on this film to do that character. I wanted him to be something no one had ever seen," says Muren. "A lot of CG stuff I had seen up until then didn't really work. But was the problem the technology or was the problem the direction? Did they not know they needed to change the brightness and make sure the shadows looked correct, or could the tools not do these things? From *Sherlock*, I found out it was a combination of both, but you could pretty much work around anything if you could clearly specify the solution."

As the hardware and software capabilities of computers improved, so too did Muren's confidence in digital effects work being used in addition to traditional techniques. The result was a succession of "huge" CG films for ILM with *The Abyss*, *Terminator 2: Judgment Day*, and *Jurassic Park*—not in terms of the CG shot counts in those films, but their impact on the industry.

For Muren, the advent of these new digital tools did not necessarily change his approach to visual effects.

[1] Dennis Muren.

[2] The stained-glass knight from **Young Sherlock Holmes**, a film for which Muren received one of his numerous visual effects Oscar nominations. The supervisor was also the first VFX artist to be honored with a Star on the Hollywood Walk of Fame.

"I like the idea of the whole movie, not just the effects shot," he says. "The effects shot in my mind should not overpower the moment. It should satisfy what the director wants at that point in the film, but it shouldn't look like an effects shot and be bigger than is possible."

"I was always very sensitive to those things," he adds. "When I was growing up watching films, I could often tell if an effects shot was coming up. I just always thought that part of the job was to make shots as seamless as they can be within the movie, so they all looked like they were shot by the same people at the same time. You're telling a story and as a viewer I don't want to be pulled out of the story."

Star Wars: Episode VI—Return of the Jedi

For the third outing of George Lucas' original *Star Wars* trilogy, *Return of the Jedi*, Muren quickly gravitated to the speeder bike chase on the forest moon of Endor, perhaps one of the most exhilarating sequences from the space saga. In these shots, Luke Skywalker (Mark Hamill) and Princess Leia (Carrie Fisher) attempt to outrun several scout troopers on the hovering bikes that are traveling at around 120-mph through the dense forest.

The final shots were realized as a combination of live-action background plates and riders shot against bluescreen, but not before several other methods had been considered. "With the weather in Northern California and the way ILM was set up at the time," says Muren, "there was some pressure to do that with miniatures and to build a forest model set. I didn't think that was a good idea because the rest of the Endor sequences were shot in locations around North Cal. and we would have needed an enormous model. I thought that if we could figure out how to do the backgrounds at least with a real forest it would just look better. It would give the sequence a sense of energy and reality."

Muren and his team scouted redwood forest locations, then produced animatics for the chase based on storyboards. "It worked out that we'd need to do about 100 shots," says Muren. "I disassembled that to show how many side and rear views there were, and really there were only about four or five different camera angles in that whole sequence."

The next challenge was working out how to acquire those angles. Muren deemed side views a relatively easy exercise involving filming the forest rushing by from a camera truck, with some wider static shots as part of the sequence as the bikes whizz through the frame. However, POV shots going straight ahead and straight behind were harder to conceive. "The point of the chase is that it has to look dangerous," explains Muren. "So it couldn't be going along a road or trail—it had to look like virgin forest."

"So we came up with the idea of using a Steadicam and walking through the forest to film it. I actually got Garrett Brown, who invented the Steadicam, involved because we needed the best mind to figure out how to walk smoothly across 1,000 feet of old growth forest floor. Garrett would shoot at about one frame per second, and when this was played back at normal projection speed of 24 frames per second it appeared as if the forest was moving past us 24x faster than the speed he'd been walking at."

For other shots on Endor, including the Ewok battle against the Imperial forces, Muren did make use of miniatures to replicate tall trees, Imperial Walkers, and tree trunk attacks. "Right before *Jedi* we did a miniature forest scene in *E.T.* for where the bicycles land," says Muren. "The ILM model shop guys made these pine trees but when I checked them out I thought they didn't look quite right. I eventually took the lead model maker up to a mountain area and we took a couple of the little trees and drove around looking at the real ones and right away you could see what was wrong with the models. Real trees go through an aging process—leaves fall off, branches fall off, branches die, there are brown areas, they are all different shapes and colors because they've gone through years of dry and wet weather. They're not your memory of trees necessarily, so I realized your memory always fails, always simplifies."

"So when we got into doing the other shots in *Jedi* with the scout walkers in the forest, I had been up there shooting the backgrounds with the actors, so I pretty much knew what a real forest looked like. I shot a lot of photos and the miniature guys and the matte painting guys looked at these as well. That philosophy of looking at references is something I've always believed in."

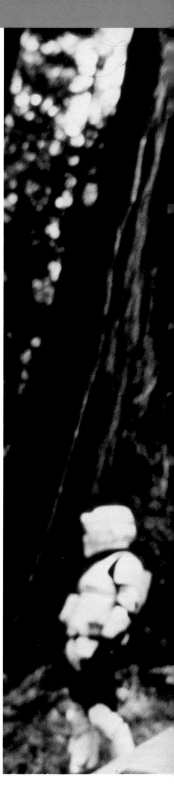

[1] Principal photography for the speeder bike scenes was filmed in redwood forest locations in California.

Terminator 2: Judgment Day

ILM had made waves in the visual effects industry with James Cameron's *The Abyss* and its CG pseudopod, but that feat would be completely overshadowed by the studio's monumental work on the director's next film—*Terminator 2: Judgment Day* (1991). The film's villain was the T-1000, a morphing, liquid-metal killing machine that was capable of shape-shifting into almost anything. Muren's approach to the look of this central and fantastical character was to still infuse the effects with an air of reality.

"Jim Cameron originally said he wanted this chrome to be 100 percent reflective," recalls Muren. "I thought to myself, 'Well, that'll look fake.' You never see anything like that—chrome on the cars, the finest diamonds, nothing is 100 percent. A mirror is not 100 percent reflective, and glass is not 100 percent transmissive—the mechanics of making those things subtracts something from it. So, of course, when we did it in the computer I clouded everything up so that the surface of our figure had a little flash level to it. It was 98 percent of a reflection, but it

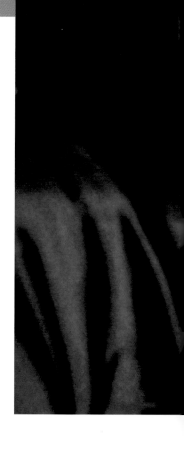

had the sense of reflecting on an object of some sort. I think that made all the difference."

"I did the same thing in *The Abyss*," adds Muren, "which was also fogged up a little. That's one of the dangers of CG—you can make it perfect, but the world isn't perfect. And what does perfect mean? You can make something 100 percent translucent or 100 percent reflective, but that's not 'perfect'—that's just 100 percent. If you really want to do something perfect, you need to match reality as best you can."

Terminator 2: Judgment Day advanced the art in ILM's animation, paint, and rendering tools. To animate shots of the T-1000 in full chrome form, effects artists actually painted a black grid on actor Robert Patrick, using the reference footage to produce a matching digital skeleton that was close to his actual gait. ILM also developed a tool called "Body Sock," which smoothed out and blended together the edges of 3D models, overcoming the problem of having intersecting creases overlapping in the CG model.

[1]

[1] The T-1000 emerges from a checkered floor. ILM created a new piece of software called "Make Sticky" to project 2D images from live-action plates onto CG models and have those images move with the model.

[2] Computer graphics and morphing techniques allowed a CG model of the T-1000 to meld into human form and have a liquid-chrome appearance. Here it enters a helicopter and morphs into the policeman form. "Jim Cameron and his guys had done very specific storyboards for how they wanted this thing to move and the shape it would be in every shot," says Muren. "We made sure it had a nice sense of viscosity and weight to it considering how heavy this thing should be in real life."

Terminator 2: Judgment Day also served as the first full show the studio did with all-digital compositing, made possible by a new digital film scanner and film output recorder. "That meant there were no matte lines suddenly that used to tip-off effects shots," notes Muren. "There was no change in the grain or resolution of anything that bothered anybody. So I think the combination of an amazingly real shape-shifting character and the invisible compositing—the way he fitted perfectly into the scenes—pretty much shocked everybody and they didn't know where to begin to critique how they might do it themselves."

Similarly, Muren ensured that ILM's digital effects closely matched the practical effects for the film created by Stan Winston—the shot of the T-1000 piercing Sarah Connor's (Linda Hamilton) shoulder with its chrome spike, for example. "The practical gag of the spike in her shoulder is Stan Winston, while we did the CG spike growing out of the hand beforehand," says Muren. "I'd look at that footage of the real spike and we'd analyze the hell out of that and make sure ours looked exactly the same. We also had to think about the physical

constraints that are put onto the real movie crew, and our shot had to include these constraints in order to cut perfectly with the preceding and following shots. Then we could finally add the best parts: dramatic lighting, movement, and creepiness."

Jurassic Park

If *Terminator 2: Judgment Day* had awoken the film industry to the possibilities of computer graphics in visual effects, then Steven Spielberg's *Jurassic Park* (1993) solidified it completely. Now, fully digital animated creatures, with lifelike skin, realistic movement, and motion blur were possible. But this was not the director's initial intention for the "full motion" dinosaur shots—Spielberg had originally tapped visual effects supervisor Phil Tippett to use his studio's stop-motion expertise for the dinosaurs. This was until some of ILM's artists somewhat secretly embarked on a CG solution.

"I thought we maybe could do a stampede sequence with our CG tools," recalls Muren, "and that wouldn't conflict with the work Phil had been awarded. But some of the guys here—Steve Williams and Mark Dippé—were pushing to do more than that. They did a test of a walking tyrannosaurus—it was just so great to see how a fluid,

walking skeleton of a T-Rex would move. You just hadn't seen anything like this before."

"I'd seen fluid performances in animation before," notes Muren, "but really this T-Rex was one of the best things I'd ever seen. However, I'd never seen any CG skin look 100 per cent real, and I'd never seen skin that appeared as though it was actually being lit by sunlight. So, although we could do animation, my worries were getting it all to come together and then delivering the movie on budget and on-time. I thought that with a combination of Phil's shop and our shop, we had a good chance."

ILM and Tippett Studio would ultimately combine forces to deliver the animation for the key dinosaurs, including the tyrannosaurus and velociraptors, while again integrating and intercutting this work with practical creatures built by Stan Winston's team.

[1] A Gallimimus herd flock towards Alan Grant (Sam Neil). The scene was filmed with tracking markers on the ground, which ILM used to help place its CG dinosaurs galloping past the actors.

[1]

[2] A herd of stegosaurus pass through in **The Lost World: Jurassic Park**. ILM enhanced its tools for high-definition skin textures and muscle deformation to create the dinosaurs for the sequel.

Heralding a new era in digital creatures, *Jurassic Park*, says Muren, proved that CG could give filmmakers more freedom in telling their stories. "I was pushing for the CG to work because I wanted to do things that were more natural looking and had regular camera movements that looked more like real-world photography. I like real movies with real actors in phenomenal situations of spectacle. I've just always been looking for stuff like that—in my home movies I was always trying things that other kids making films weren't trying."

Muren also supervised the visual effects for Spielberg's *Jurassic Park* follow-up, *The Lost World: Jurassic Park* (1997). By that time, ILM had continued refining its computer graphics pipeline and made headway on adding details such as skin sliding over digital muscles and bones. "I like the variation in that show a lot," states Muren. "The tiny compy creatures, the stuff in San Diego, the T-Rex at night, the lighting, the animation—I think it's a very cool dinosaur movie, with the creature ending up back in the city destroying things, which is what you want to see!"

A.I. Artificial Intelligence

Re-teaming with Steven Spielberg on *A.I. Artificial Intelligence* (2001), Muren introduced a new innovation into film visual effects by implementing a real-time, on-set visualization system for the Rogue City sequences completed by ILM. This allowed the filmmakers to see live composites of the actors against CG backgrounds and thus compose previews of final shots.

Muren had witnessed such live-tracking technologies in television broadcasts. "I'd seen some TV news shows and sport shows where you could see there was real-time camera tracking going on," he says. "You'd see the newscaster standing in an amazing set, but he was actually bluescreened onto a CG. The camera was just panning around in any direction, which was pretty much impossible and unaffordable in bluescreen composite shots for feature films. So I thought this would be a great tool for the director or the DOP or for me to be able to plan the shot in advance by actually seeing it on the set, or maybe see it in a real shot."

The system began by acquiring camera motions from a live video camera attached to the filming camera. The video photographed patterned disks on the ceiling of the bluescreen stage. Using the patterns, machine-vision software created trajectory camera data that copied these movements onto the virtual camera "viewing" the rendered CG background. This background was

[1] Actors Jude Law and Haley Joel Osment are filmed on a bluescreen stage.

[2] Another layer to the shot: digital buildings.

[3] The final composite, which also features a mid-ground miniature building and additional CG elements.

simply matted behind the actor's live camera feed. "On the set we were set up cable-less so the DOP, Janusz Kaminski, and Steven could just move the camera anywhere they wanted and nobody would have to be worried about tripping over anything," says Muren. "I thought it was a miracle! You wouldn't have to use your mind's eye anymore. I thought it would be really helpful for the cameraman to be able to see what the lighting would be in the background also, if you got it that far along and rendered nicely. It was really a way to get the DOP involved in CG sets and lighting."

Although the system was successful, it was not immediately adopted by the visual-effects industry.

"I thought it was going to have a big future," admits Muren, "but like other things it just didn't because I don't think people saw an advantage in it until these big CG shows came along like *Avatar*. For that film, they really needed something close to real time, which at the time we had, but the geometry was very simple in 2000. Of course, now this is used all the time for previs and on set with the idea of being able to frame your shot up and lock your angle."

War of the Worlds

Steven Spielberg's *War of the Worlds* (2005) was a film that Muren says fulfilled his "ultimate dream" as a visual effects supervisor at ILM. "It represented my love for documentary, but with Hollywood photography. I love that fluid camera and the mixing of lenses in sequences because they just look very real."

Indeed, the movie follows father Ray Ferrier (Tom Cruise) and his family on the run from alien tripods, often using hand-held cameras to put the audience close to the action. "It gives the audience this feeling that they are actually there with Tom, seeing things from his point of view," says Muren. "Very seldom are you at a God's point of view—you're experiencing and learning things at the same time and same camera height as Tom is learning it. That was all very intentional in the show."

A shot that is typical of the production—and Muren's desire to keep it as real as possible—was a long take following people as they attempt to escape the giant tripod's vaporizing beams. "When they blow up they turn to smoke and you see all these clothes flying all over the place," describes Muren. "That could have been done by filming backgrounds shot on location, matting in people running in front of a bluescreen, and covering the switch with the explosion effect. But I just thought that's not what you want to do to make it feel real. For me, if you aren't feeling the shot, it's not working. And every shot presents that opportunity."

"So for those takes," continues Muren, "I had the actors running through the street and just fall down without getting hurt and just stay there and not move anymore. More and more people fall, the take just

[1] Alien tripods make their presence known.

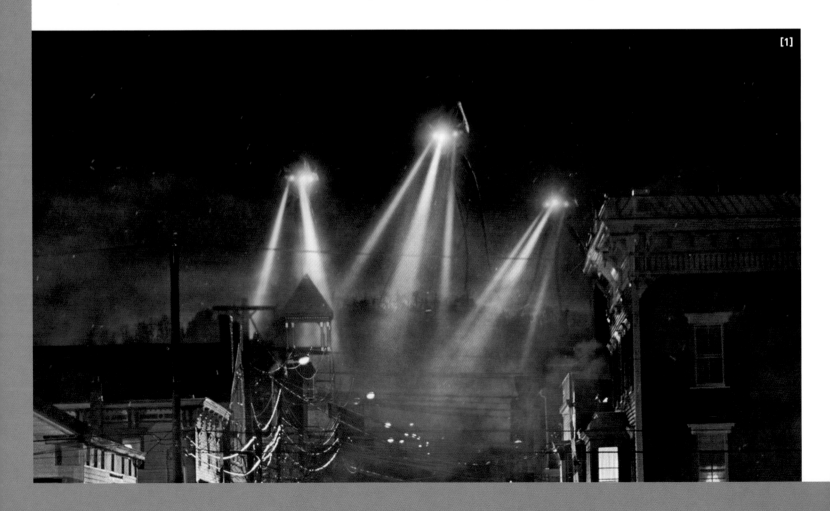

[1]

[2]

[2] Appearing unexpectedly in New Jersey, an alien tripod prepares to attack. ILM's visual effects for the film had to adapt to Spielberg's documentary, human height, long-take approach.

[3] A giant tripod readies an attack on an escaping ship.

keeps going on and on and we get our 20-second shot. We would then go in and paint them out digitally from that frame onward and replace that with a real smoke element or real clothes flying up in the air, or CG smoke or dust. The idea is that shot is absolutely real until the effect pops on and from then on you're seeing an effect."

Where buildings and vehicles are blown apart by the tripods, ILM captured background plates and then photographed exploding miniatures with static cameras and tracked those into the live-action plates. "That meant that right up until the destruction, it's all absolutely real," says Muren. "There's no clue you're seeing an effects shot. We gave Steven full freedom to do whatever he wanted to do with the camera, to pan around everywhere."

12 > John Rosengrant

One of the perks of working in the effects industry may be the ability to contribute to iconic film characters, and John Rosengrant has contributed to many. The creature and makeup effects supervisor has worked on the iconic T-800 and T-100 characters in *The Terminator* films, the alien queen from *Aliens*, the T-Rex's and velociraptors of the *Jurassic Park* series, the suits in the *Iron Man* films, the Na'vi and mechanical craft of *Avatar*, and the robots for *Real Steel*, for which he received a visual effects Oscar nomination.

Coming to Los Angeles in the early 1980s, after studying Fine Arts at Louisiana State University, Rosengrant would soon be working with distinguished practical effects artist Stan Winston. An Oscar winner for *Aliens*, *Jurassic Park*, and *Terminator 2: Judgment Day*, the revered Winston passed away in 2008 after years collaborating with Rosengrant, who has continued the tradition of practical effects work via his company, Legacy Effects.

"Stan was an amazing artist, businessman, mentor, and friend," says Rosengrant. "I feel really fortunate to have had such an amazing career opportunity starting with Stan. Personally, I have high standards for the work that we do, which fits in perfectly with Stan's approach. Stan Winston Studio was always searching for ways to make the work better and at Legacy Effects we maintain that tradition and continue to push the boundaries."

Rosengrant's unique skills lie in helping filmmakers realize their visions on screen and, in particular, in providing a practical basis for filmed characters and effects. "My art is very collaborative, as is filmmaking, and our area of expertise encompasses design, fabrication, and on-set performance," he explains. "We are in the business of creating iconic characters and it's those three disciplines that need to come together to make that character come alive. Each phase is extremely and equally important—a beautiful concept that cannot realistically perform is a failure, and vice versa."

"The middle step of the actual creation of the piece, the fabrication, involves many important sub-steps if it's a practical or digital effect," adds Rosengrant. "In the practical world it's either a rapid prototyped piece, as in

the case of an *Iron Man* suit or a robot from *Real Steel*, or it could be a traditional hand-sculpted character. The steps that follow are mold-making, casting the pieces, fabrication, and mechanizing. If it's a makeup design or character, the same steps would basically apply."

As a practical creature-effects creator in an increasingly digital world, Rosengrant says his company has "never been shy about embracing new technologies. All digital can be detectable, as can all practical. Hybrid shots are terrific in that they encompass both techniques. *A.I. Artificial Intelligence* and *Terminator 3: Rise of the Machines* were great early examples of that combination as far as makeup goes, as you can only build out with traditional makeup. But combining with CG, to take away, is a game changer. As makeup designers, it adds a freedom that we never had in the old days. The same thought process works with animatronics where we've augmented puppets or suits like the ones we did for *Total Recall* and *RoboCop*, where you digitally augment by making something thinner than it could be."

[1] John Rosengrant sits in the cockpit of an Amp Suit constructed by Legacy Effects for **Avatar**.

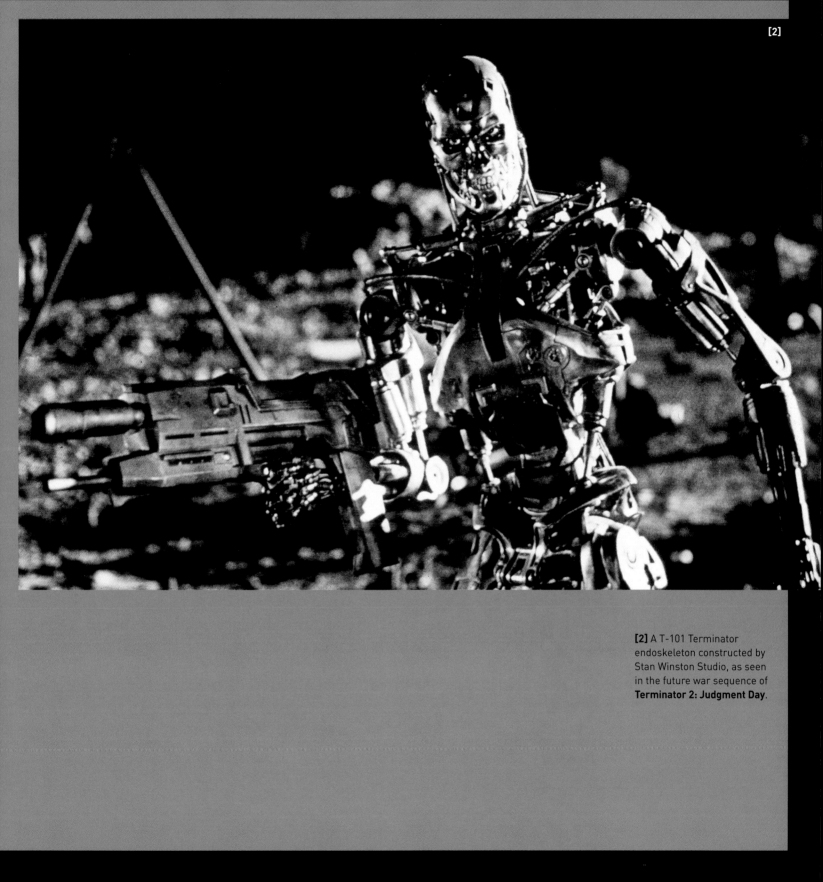

[2] A T-101 Terminator endoskeleton constructed by Stan Winston Studio, as seen in the future war sequence of **Terminator 2: Judgment Day**.

The Terminator and Terminator 2: Judgment Day

James Cameron's *The Terminator* (1984), was Rosengrant's first major special effects film credit. "When we were working on it," he says, "it felt like it was going to be something special. It just had that kind of energy about it." Indeed, the relatively low-budget action film that mixed practical builds, miniature effects, rear projection, and optical effects, made Cameron a household name and established the Stan Winston team as forerunners in effects creation and collaboration.

Rosengrant's work ranged from makeup gags to metal endoskeleton builds, with effects having to be rapidly deployed on each day of filming. "We pulled a lot of all nighters getting things ready," recalls Rosengrant. "The famous scene where the Terminator cuts out his

eyeball, I remember that shot moving up in the schedule and having to quickly make the eyeball that gets tossed in the sink out of a gelatine material. I worried it would not look good, until I saw the film, and it always gets a big reaction—a good reaction, that is."

Another signature shot was of the Terminator endoskeleton being crushed in a press at the end of the film. "The crushable endo didn't flatten down quite enough," says Rosengrant, "so I actually found some heavy duty foil the grips had and very quickly fabricated part of the skull in foil. That became the last image of him you see in the press."

The return of Arnold Schwarzenegger as the T-800 in *Terminator 2: Judgment Day* (1991) saw with it an

[1] Shot with a grenade, the T-1000 implodes. The effect was an animatronic puppet that could be articulated on set to full effect.

[1]

advancement in practical, makeup, and animatronic creature effects, and a new association with digital effects work. One of Rosengrant's favorite creations on the film, however, was one he says most people think is CG, but isn't. "It's the frozen T-1000 being shot by the Terminator and shattering into a million pieces. That was 100 per cent practical. The frozen T-1000 was a hollow casting in fiberglass, pre-scored, with explosive primer cord wrapped inside blown up on set. There was also fine metallic confetti inside to add to the effect."

In the film's stunning climax, the liquid metal T-1000 is blown up with a grenade launcher before meeting its doom by falling into a vat of molten steel. Damaged by the grenade, the still standing but splattered T-1000 was dubbed "Pretzel Man" by the creature effects crew. "There were three Pretzel Man puppets," explains Rosengrant. "One that was folded up and was rigged to explode and splay open, with its head driven upward by a pneumatic ram. Then it was a cut to the hero animatronic puppet, which we called Stage 2."

"There was a gimbal in each ankle," continues Rosengrant, "with a rod running up the legs that provided that wonky, dazed gross body motion by puppeteers below it, out of the shot. The head had radio control jaw and eye movement. Driving the gross head movement was a cable-controlled rotor that allowed it to spin around back to camera. The third puppet was unarticulated, just a reactive floppy piece that had weights in it to help it fall into the molten steel pit, which was made of methyl-cellulose."

Rosengrant's association with *The Terminator* franchise has continued with Jonathan Mostow's *Terminator 3: Rise of the Machines* (2003), and McG's *Terminator Salvation* (2009), with each film showcasing continued innovation in makeup appliances, full-sized robots, and endoskeletons.

[2] Arnold Schwarzenegger, as the Terminator, repairs his own endoskeleton— beneath a prosthetic arm makeup appliance.

Jurassic Park

For Steven Spielberg's groundbreaking *Jurassic Park* (1993), Rosengrant worked with the team at Stan Winston Studio to deliver full-sized animatronic dinosaurs, smaller insert puppets, and part-puppets. But it was Rosengrant's stint inside a velociraptor suit for the film's kitchen sequence that was his most memorable contribution.

"That was a really interesting experience that required both physical training and acting," he recalls. "I studied several different types of animals ranging from large birds to lizards to inform the movement. I worked out with a trainer for several months before shooting to be prepared physically—suits like this are tough, as they put a strain on your body and endurance." Rosengrant was first envisaged inside the raptor via pencil drawings depicting the dinosaur with the artist inside. A body cast

taken of Rosengrant then ensured that the correct shape of the creature could be sculpted around him— even a miniature clay sculpt was made to check that the configuration would work.

Before a final velociraptor suit was constructed, however, it was made in foam pieces over Rosengrant's life cast to test the fit. Dubbed the "garbage bag test," the foam appliances would allow Rosengrant to rehearse in the suit. Specifically, he followed storyboards and animatics that had been created by Phil Tippett for the kitchen scene. It also ensured he could stand for sometimes four hours at a time in a "ski pose," slightly bending at the waist. When the foam latex suit was completed, painted, and dressed onto Rosengrant, the strenuous shooting could begin. "These suits are very

[1] The team from Stan Winston Studio build a full-scale animatronic tyrannosaurus.

[2] John Rosengrant wore a velociraptor suit for shots in the kitchen sequence, scenes that made use of both practical and digital effects. The practical raptor skin was constructed from foam rubber made from a mix of air and liquid latex rubber left to cure in a mold.

hot inside and your visibility is severely limited," states Rosengrant, "so it almost becomes physical acting by muscle memory based on extensive rehearsals."

The full-sized suit and various extension and insert suit pieces were used for specific views and others were realized via computer graphics. Rosengrant brought to life the classic toe-tapping shot, for example. "Based on the storyboards," he adds, "I also came up with a routine for when the raptor enters the kitchen and hoots for the other one to enter and that's what I did on the day. Fortunately it worked out well and made it to the film!"

As more *Jurassic Park* films were made, Rosengrant again performed inside raptor suits and contributed to full-scale dino effects, such as the two T-Rex's in *The Lost World: Jurassic Park* (1997) and the spinosaurus in *Jurassic Park III* (2001)

Iron Man

On Jon Favreau's *Iron Man* (2008)—and subsequent films in the Marvel superhero franchise—Rosengrant and his colleagues at the then Stan Winston Studio would further the art of on-set practical effects. "We worked very closely with the Marvel team on these suits," says Rosengrant. "There was a lot of back and forth, particularly on the very first suit, getting it designed to look great and be functional."

Shane Mahan, a Legacy Effects co-founder, would lead the charge at Stan Winston in crafting a suit—the classic automotive red gold Mark III suit worn by Tony

[1] Ivan Vanko (Mickey Rourke) wears the Whiplash suit in **Iron Man 2**, which he uses to battle Tony Stark.

[2] Robert Downey Jr. wears the Mark III suit in **Iron Man**. A mix of full metallic-looking suits, partial suits, and CG recreations made up the final shots in the film.

[3]

[3] The Mark I suit used by Tony Stark to escape an Afghanistan cave. A new metallic painting technique applied to the suit to provide a unique reflective quality would become the go-to method for suit work at Stan Winston Studio and Legacy Effects.

Stark (Robert Downey Jr.). However, suit construction had to be commenced before Downey Jr. was cast in the role. To do this, Legacy Effects computer-designed suit parts and then cast them via rapid prototyping.

On set, Downey Jr. or a stuntman would wear full or partial builds of the practical suit, with digital visual effects also playing a role in delivering Iron Man performances. "On the first film," explains Rosengrant, "there were several full head-to-toe suits. The key is working on top of a real human form, someone as close to the classic '8 head tall' heroic proportion and finding that balance to make it functional and esthetically pleasing. I think the reality of it, really working, transfers through in the believability. It's become our standard practice in building these type of suits."

Stan Winston Studio also built the Mark I suit—the first suit seen in the film that Stark constructs to help

him escape from a cave in Afghanistan. With more of a rustic, bulky, "tin can" look, the 90-pound Mark I also incorporated deliberate hammer damage, bullet holes, and wear and tear to its chrome finish.

In the subsequent *Iron Man* films, Legacy Effects would go on to make further suits, drones, and actor Mickey Rourke's Whiplash suit, as seen in *Iron Man 2*. Often these creations would be inter-mixed between other practical and digital effects. "My philosophy," comments Rosengrant, "has always been that whatever methodology is best for the shot is the needed approach, whether practical or digital, even though I make a living in the practical world of effects I personally think to mix the two types of effects together, taking advantage of what both methods have to offer, keeps the audience off balance and unsure what they are looking at."

Real Steel

Shawn Levy's *Real Steel* (2011) tells the near-future story where robot boxing is one of the most popular spectator sports. The eight-foot tall robots in the film were realized as both practical boxing robots overseen by Rosengrant at Legacy Effects and digital robots made by the visual effects team from Digital Domain. "*Real Steel* was a great film for us on a lot of levels," says Rosengrant. "It was, I felt, a beautiful blend of computer-generated and animatronic characters."

Although certain scenes were always planned as sequences that would make use of full-motion CG robots, Legacy's creations could be positioned on set. Here they served as excellent lighting and texture reference that could inform digital artists on how reflections, shadows, and lights might bounce off the metallic surfaces when the artists created their own versions of the robots.

Designing the robots was a six-month process involving rapid prototyping and piecing together around 300 parts for each robot. "Our use of various computer sculpting and engineering programs allowed us direct interface with our mechanical department engineering team, pre-building in the placement of the mechanical components," recounts Rosengrant. "This enabled a streamlined build on the back end during the construction phase, with the animatronics dropping into place. It also gave us range of motion tests to see if any shells or other components would crash into each other."

The final practical robots were predominantly built from panels of fiberglass and urethane, while their internal mechanical parts relied on steel and aluminum. On set, the robots could be operated via a hydraulically motivated, actor-puppeteered control system by a Legacy Effects crew member.

Ultimately, Legacy Effects made 27 robots for the film, some for close interaction with the actors and others as background characters. "We also made some for scenes that would be difficult to pull off in CG," explains Rosengrant, "such as Atom coming back to life, mud and dust coated, sitting up with real dried mud

[1] After discovering the boxing robot Atom in a junkyard, Charlie Kenton (Hugh Jackman) and his son Max (Dakota Goyo) bring him back to life in Bailey Tallet's (Evangeline Lilly) workshop.

and bits falling off. Another scene entailed the young
actor washing the mud off Atom."

A further practical creation for on-set use was Noisy
Boy, a samurai-style robot that Legacy infused with
around 2,000 LED lights showing random Japanese
sayings on its forearm.

The result of having robots such as Atom and Noisy
Boy on location, says Rosengrant, was a "tactile quality,
an actual in-the-scene feeling" to the shots. "The practical
robots provide not only a visual reference for an actor,
but something to actually perform with. Having on-set
robots for the young actor to act with was essential. To
quote Shawn Levy: 'Not only did the real robot establish
a benchmark for the digital effects, but it also lent a
reality to the performances that you simply do not get
when you ask an actor to do a scene with a tennis ball
on a stick. And when that actor is a ten-year-old boy,
the magic that happens in his eyes when he's face to
face with a real moving robot is invaluable.'"

[2] Having a practical Atom
robot on set helped inform
the digital visual effects
artists when it came to
creating a CG version
for full-motion shots.

[3] Charlie instructs Noisy
Boy on his next fight.

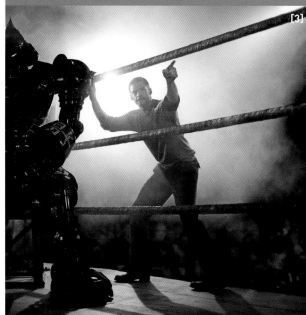

13 > Phil Tippett

Phil Tippett has brought life to some of the most well-known and loved characters and creatures in recent film memory—the AT-AT walkers and Tauntauns in *Star Wars: Episode VI—The Empire Strikes Back*, the lumbering ED-209 from *RoboCop*, the breakthrough dinosaurs in *Jurassic Park*, the bugs of *Starship Troopers*, and more recently, the wolves in *The Twilight Saga*.

[1] Phil Tippett works on a stop-motion figure.

However, the stop-motion and visual effects pioneer once thought his career had come to a grinding halt, when, during the production of Steven Spielberg's *Jurassic Park*, he saw the capabilities of the then-new computer-generated imagery and animation in film.

Yet rather than stalling, Tippett drew on his expertise in hand-animation work and embraced the digital domain, becoming one of the go-to effects artists in Hollywood for creatures. Indeed, he has won two visual effects Academy Awards (*Star Wars: Episode VI—Return of the Jedi* and *Jurassic Park*) and been nominated for an Oscar a further four times (*Dragonslayer*, *Willow*, *DragonHeart*, and *Starship Troopers*).

After attending University of California, Irvine, and then working as an animator at Cascade Pictures in Los Angeles, Tippett was recruited into the effects team for the George Lucas' 1977 space opera, *Star Wars: Episode IV—A New Hope*. Here he would help to flesh out the aliens in the cantina sequence and the holographic chess pieces on board the Millennium Falcon.

Star Wars ushered in a new era of visual effects wizardry, and while working at Lucas' Industrial Light & Magic (ILM) Tippett continued to innovate on subsequent films in the franchise, as well as other projects. On Matthew Robbins' *Dragonslayer*, he helped pioneer a stop-motion process dubbed Go Motion that brought "motion blur" and thus more realistic-looking animation to creature effects.

Go Motion helped solve one of the problems inherent with the established practice of stop motion, that of the apparent "sharpness" of the image on film. This is because the very nature of stop frame animation is a still image for each frame. Even when played back at 24 frames per second, a stop-motion animated character tended to exhibit a certain level of jerkiness since there

is no motion blur, something that would normally be recorded in live action. Go Motion, instead, brought motion blur into stop-motion animation by enabling the puppet to move while each frame of the film was being exposed. The technique worked by articulating an animation puppet with computer-controlled rods that could move along the X, Y, and Z axes. It was a technology with origins in the motion-control camera equipment Tippett had witnessed being used on the first *Star Wars* film at ILM for the space battles. The added benefit was that, since the puppet's movements could be computer programmed, the animation could be repeated, expanded, or sped up to achieve a desired look without having to start over.

After *Jurassic Park*'s further wave of computerized visual effects innovations, Tippett recognized the industry shift and moved Tippett Studio into the digital realm, taking on the challenging bugs in Paul Verhoeven's *Starship Troopers*. Since then, he has overseen creature animation in numerous films, such as the trolls and goblins of Mark Waters' *The Spiderwick Chronicles* and the shape-shifting wolves from *The Twilight Saga*.

Few other practitioners have had the opportunity to work on so many seminal effects productions, and even fewer have spanned the relatively enormous jump from practical to digital. However, Tippett suggests that he and several other now-legendary visual effects supervisors landed "in the right place at the right time," when directors such as George Lucas and Steven Spielberg wanted to make fantasy and sci-fi films, and there simply were not that many artists doing the effects work required. "We just got lucky," he says.

[2] A final shot of the AT-ATs launching their attack on the rebel base on the ice planet Hoth in **Star Wars: Episode V—The Empire Strikes Back**.

[3] Phil Tippett animates an AT-AT. "The Walkers were something no animator in their right mind would design, just because of their long legs," says Tippett. "However, we were able to get great reference from elephants and other creatures for how they should move."

The original Star Wars trilogy

Among the many contributions Phil Tippett made to George Lucas' original *Star Wars* trilogy were the miniature creatures for the holographic chess sequence in *Star Wars: Episode IV—A New Hope*. "George had wanted to do the chess scene as live-action people with masks on," recalls Tippett, "but another movie had a similar hologram so he suggested doing it in stop motion. We knocked out some of these creatures in less than a week, and used some of the puppets I had made already from past experiments. Then we went in and shot at it over a couple of days."

Having impressed the director with these alien designs and his animation skills, Tippett, along with Jon Berg and Dennis Muren, was called upon to animate the almost elephant-like AT-AT walkers and the Tauntauns on the ice planet of Hoth in *Star Wars: Episode V—The Empire Strikes Back*. The meticulous frame-by-frame approach took advantage of the motion-control equipment developed for the first *Star Wars* film—the result was that helicopter-like camera moves could be achieved on the walkers and Tauntauns within the snowy environment.

To illustrate how a puppet could be animated with realistic motion blur, Tippett tested the shot first with an existing model he had made for Joe Dante's *Piranha* (1978). Sweeping moves on Hoth were realized with motion-control cameras, computer controlled so that

[1] The Rancor in **Star Wars: Episode VI—Return of the Jedi**. "Initially," says Tippett, "George wanted to do a man in a suit. I was in charge of on-set and live-action creatures for the Jabba the Hutt scene, so some of the guys back at the shop at ILM started building a suit a performer could wear based on my designs. But it wasn't really working. In the end, George said, 'Oh do whatever you want to do!'"

[1]

[2] Phil Tippett adds final touches to the Rancor puppet seen in **Star Wars: Episode VI—Return of the Jedi**.

multiple passes could be filmed and optically composited. "These motion-control rigs were already there for the space battles, so we figured out ways of using the forward momentum to get the motion blur when the camera shutter was open," explains Tippett.

On *Star Wars: Episode VI—Return of the Jedi*, Tippett designed the Rancor, a fearsome creature living in the dungeon of Jabba the Hutt's palace. It was operated as a hand-and-rod puppet, with Tippett controlling the head from underneath a miniature set, while others controlled its hands with bicycle brake-type levers. "We shot everything at between 72- and 96-frames per second, so the takes were really fast," says Tippett. "What was going to show up on the screen was only four seconds, so it had to be shot in less than two seconds. Sometimes we would shoot 70 takes."

RoboCop

Although Tippett had advanced the art of stop-motion animation with Go Motion while working on *Dragonslayer*, Paul Verhoeven's *RoboCop* (1987) saw a "throwback" to more traditional hand-animated work with effects for the film's fully automated (but ill-fated) peacekeeping machine called ED-209.

A full, life-size prop of the robot was designed and constructed by Craig Hayes and used on set, with Tippett animating a miniature ED-209 for scenes requiring it to walk. "We also did everything much more small-scale using split screens and rear projection, and put it together just like animator Ray Harryhausen would

have done on films like *Jason and the Argonauts* (1963)," says Tippett. "Plus ED-209 was a robot, so it leant itself to linear stop motion."

Inside the ED-209 model was a stop-motion metal armature that allowed movement, surrounded by a vacuformed plastic shell. Animators introduced motion blur into shots by slightly "wiggling" the models as each frame of film was exposed, and relied on a double-pass in-camera technique for muzzle flashes when ED-209 fired its weapons.

RoboCop not only represented an opportunity for Tippett to return to his stop-motion beginnings, but also to instill

[1]

a high degree of personality into what was essentially an industrial machine. "For example," Tippett recalls, "I was getting set up to do the final shot of ED-209 having his head blown off by RoboCop when I got a call from the film's producer who said, 'We just screened the film, and we need a laugh—do something funny'. So I did—I made him teeter like a drunk person and fall over and have his foot twitch a little."

Tippett would follow up his work on the first *RoboCop* film with more stop-motion animation for *RoboCop 2* (1990) and *RoboCop 3* (1993), delivering the memorable prototypes and Cain robot.

[1] A final shot from the boardroom sequence in **RoboCop**, in which the fully automated ED-209 robot is demonstrated to disastrous effect. To replicate the live-action setting, Tippett Studio constructed a replica set that included the harsh corporate lighting.

[2] A Tippett Studio artist works on a prototype robot for **RoboCop 2**. In the final stop motion animated scene, the robot would remove its own helmet to reveal a semi-alive skull underneath.

Jurassic Park

Having mastered the art of stop motion, Tippett was one of Steven Spielberg's first considerations to bring the dinosaurs of *Jurassic Park* (1993) to life. Initially, it was envisaged shots of the creatures in full motion would be hand-animated by Tippett as Go Motion effects, then composited into background plates by ILM, who would also deliver stampede scenes using computer-generated dinosaurs. But after Spielberg saw a CG demo by ILM, the future of visual effects suddenly became apparent.

Tippett was at the test screening where his friend, ILM visual effects supervisor Dennis Muren, showed off the capabilities of photorealistic digital animation. "Steven asked me how I felt and I said, 'I feel extinct'," remembers Tippett. "He said, 'I'm going to put that in the movie!' He had Dr Grant say it at one point."

However, Tippett's experience in creature animation and a deep knowledge of paleontology ensured that he was retained in the role of "Dinosaur Supervisor"—the actual final credit. Among his contributions was a dinosaur bible outlining designs, behaviors, and walk

[1] A tyrannosaurus breaks through a gate in this scene from **Jurassic Park**. Phil Tippett oversaw the T-Rex animation, which was undertaken by Tippett Studio animators Randy Dutra and Tom St. Amand. The pair employed a digital input device that resembled a stop-motion armature with sensors that fed into a 3D-animation package. The film saw a unique collaboration between Tippett, ILM, and Stan Winston, whose practical full-scale dinosaurs were intercut directly with their CG counterparts.

[1]

[2] Velociraptors stalk Tim Murphy (Joseph Mazzello) in the kitchen. The sequence was heavily previsualized by Tippett's crew with stop-motion animatics.

cycles; stop motion animatics for the T-Rex paddock attack and velociraptor kitchen scenes; and input on the final dinosaur sound designs.

"At that particular time," says Tippett, "there weren't a lot of CG animators who were trained to do living characters. People had done TV commercials with flying logos and cartoony things, but it's a whole different world when you're trying to match your artificial characters in a photographic background plate that's shot on earth with a certain kind of lighting and specific gravity. You have to really nail it and know what you're doing to have all that stuff fit in."

Tippett Studio animators also contributed digital animation to key scenes with the aid of a digital input device developed by Craig Hayes, Rick Sayre, Brian Knep, and Thomas Williams. "This was essentially a stop-motion armature turned into a motion-capture

device," explains Tippett. "It had little encoders on it that you could plug into the computer and physically manipulate in real space, and have that duplicated inside the computer as a wire frame."

The visual effects supervisor also says that his "Dinosaur Supervisor" credit—later a source of much consternation among fans of the film, who questioned why Tippett had not done a better job of ensuring the dinosaurs didn't kill so many people—was actually part of Spielberg's "showmanship." "ILM, for example, got credit for full-motion dinosaurs and that was designed not to indicate one way or the other how it was done. Steven didn't want attention called to the technology. He just wanted the magic of seeing dinosaurs and the audience coming away and not thinking how it was done."

Starship Troopers

It was Tippett's re-teaming with Paul Verhoeven for *Starship Troopers* (1997) that pushed the visual effects supervisor and his company fully into the world of complex computer-generated imagery and animation for the distinctive bug enemies of this film.

Starship Troopers' complex work was helped by a further incarnation of the digital input device used in *Jurassic Park*, along with advancements in other animation tools. However, the film still presented many challenges, including thousands of bugs on screen at a time, explosions, and direct interaction with actors.

The show required bug enemies to be split into distinctive war groupings—ground attack warriors,

[1] John "Johnny" Rico (Casper Van Dien) tries to evade a deadly Tanker bug.

[1]

[2] Warrior bugs, know as "Arachnids," attack a military outpost. "Paul Verhoeven really wanted the bugs to have strong staccato and chaotic movements," says Tippett. To help animate the bugs, Tippett Studio built on the digital input devices first used on **Jurassic Park** to create the bug animation, and then used a swarming system to show thousands of bugs in the same scene.

aerial creatures, and even a flame-throwing tank-like bug—all of which had to be designed from the ground up.

"*Jurassic Park* in some ways was actually easier to do than *Starship Troopers* because for the movements you have a paleontological record," admits Tippett. "All the design work's been done for you. But when you're doing a fantasy character you have to back up and say, 'How does it actually work?'"

"The Brain Bug in particular was this gigantic technological hurdle that was labyrinthian," adds Tippett. "It had this quasi-translucent skin and it was moving all the time, plus it had a net on top of that. Nobody had really done anything like that before. We weren't quite sure we could either. But Craig Hayes engineered that."

Luckily, Verhoeven's satirical take on the subject matter and the copious head decapitations, impalements, and general blood and gore also suited Tippett's own sensibilities. "I actually heard that when George Lucas saw the movie he said to somebody, 'That was the job Phil was born to do.' I was always trying to get directors to chop people's heads off and squish people—George didn't like to do that kind of stuff, but Paul did."

Tippett would go on to become synonymous with the creatures of *Starship Troopers*; the visual effects supervisor directed a sequel to the film, 2004's *Starship Troopers 2: Hero of the Federation.*

The Twilight Saga

Starting with Chris Weitz's *The Twilight Saga: New Moon* (2009), Tippett oversaw the creation of several of the wolves for the film series—a task he knew immediately would be challenging.

"The first thing everybody said was that they wanted the wolves to look absolutely real," Tippett notes. "And then you have to say, 'How come you're not shooting it with real wolves?' The answer is, of course, that real wolves can't act, which is what our wolves had to do. You've got to find where on the meter the anthropomorphic crosses over with lupine behavior."

That balance required referencing both actor performances and real wolves. Tippett had animators watch hours of documentary footage and also visit a wildlife park to interact directly with timberwolves. "Once we work out the behavior, then a lot of it is technology—getting the fur to look better, for example," says Tippett.

"On each new film," he adds, "everything is usually just a prototype, figuring out how to make it all work. But having the franchise allowed us to develop better and more sophisticated ways of doing it, over a period of three or four years."

The role of visual effects became so crucial to the storytelling in the *The Twilight Saga*, that in Bill Condon's *Breaking Dawn—Part I* (2011), a lumber yard meeting

[1] For the lumber yard wolf-pack sequence in **Breaking Dawn—Part 1**, Tippett Studio animators had direct involvement in the final shots. "We got people from the company and did a repertoire reading one afternoon and we went through a bunch of temporary track music to get the emotional tone," says Tippett. "This was all going to be changed eventually, but it was essentially a rehearsal for the final movie."

[1]

[3]

[2]

The Twilight Saga: Breaking Dawn—Part 1 and The Twilight Saga: New Moon courtesy of Summit Entertainment, LLC.

The Twilight Saga: Breaking Dawn—Part 1 and The Twilight Saga: New Moon courtesy of Summit Entertainment, LLC.

[2] Jacob Black in werewolf form from **New Moon**. On set, cardboard cutouts of the wolves were used as stand-ins to reference size and framing, while "loaves" of wolf fur would be filmed in the scene to provide a lighting reference.

[3] An in-house grooming tool called "Furator" allowed the VFX artists to create realistic wolf coats. The tool enabled them to easily change various hair characteristics, including hair "scraggle."

amongst the wolf park was previsualized in rough form by Tippett and his animation team, who even provided a scratch voice track. "I've got a team of animators I've been working with for many, many years—it's like having a group of ensemble players where we all know each other really well, and I was really able to give them so much latitude to create the scene."

"My direction is usually extremely general," continues Tippett. "I'm kind of influenced more by live-action production work than actual animation work where everything has to be very specific. If you know the scene and know what's required, then I'll say to the animator, 'Here's the scene, in this particular shot the wolf has to go from here to here and he looks back at the other character...and I'll see you tomorrow!'"

14 > Douglas Trumbull

In 1968, Stanley Kubrick's *2001: A Space Odyssey* changed the landscape of science-fiction filmmaking with its serious contemplation of man and the meaning of life. At the same time, the film's incredible imagery—both on Earth and in outer space—also changed the landscape of visual effects. As a special photographic effects supervisor on the film, Douglas Trumbull was a key part of that equation. He would continue to utilize innovative effects solutions in films such as *Close Encounters of the Third Kind*, *Star Trek: The Motion Picture*, and *Blade Runner*, each garnering a visual effects Academy Award nomination. Trumbull also directed *Silent Running* and *Brainstorm*, and pioneered the concept of "immersive cinema" in ride and special venue films with his Showscan technology—a cinematic process using 70mm film capturing and projecting images at 60 frames per second. More recently, Trumbull has been exploring stereo, digital, and virtual set technologies.

[1]

It is this idea of immersive cinema that Trumbull is most passionate about, and something he says he has been striving for all his life. "It's a combination of things I learned when I was working with Showscan and IMAX, and a lot of it even began with *To the Moon and Beyond*, which pre-dated *A Space Odyssey*. It was about recognizing that 24 frames per second is inadequate because there's so much blurring and strobing. I've also just recently discovered with this new digital technology that we can make something new—an opportunity for a whole new cinematic language. It's a first-person experience rather than a third-person experience."

Trumbull pushed the art of ride and special venue films both with Showscan and other adaptations of film capture and projection, often coupled with audiences sitting in a specialized theater or on motion bases tied to the action on the screen. Some of the most successful of these films included *Back to the Future—The Ride* and *Secrets of the Luxor Pyramid*.

In researching how to make these kinds of films as exhilarating for the audience as possible, Trumbull considered aspects such as frame rate, resolution, stereoscopic projection, dome screens, multi-channel sound, screen brightness, and even angle of view to the screen. "It's very well known," he says, "in the world of flight simulation that if you want to convince a pilot that he's flying you want to have a field of view that's at least

90-degrees wide if not 100- or 120-degrees wide. That's what they were trying to do in Cinerama, for example—it was a deeply curved wide screen and the result of an aircraft gunnery simulation trainer called 'Vitarama.'"

Most recently, Trumbull's goal has been to merge the immersive qualities of these kinds of films with more narrative storytelling, something he feels that digital cameras and workflows can help achieve. "My aim is to produce something where the realism is so high that each audience member feels like they are actually participating in the action on the screen," says Trumbull. "I want them to feel that they have a direct interaction with the action on the screen and feel like they have personal eye contact and that the actors are talking to the audience. Instead of the camera being a third-person observer of action, the camera can become a character and therefore each audience member can become an observer, or another character, and switch roles."

The other important qualities for immersion, adds Trumbull, can be stereo and high frame rates. While acknowledging stereo has not always been successful, and that audiences have had somewhat of an aversion to frame rates higher than 24 frames per second—the industry standard—he says that if done properly these two aspects can transport viewers more fully into a film. "When you take 3D and high frame rate and combine them on a movie that's actually a fantasy story, say,

[1] Douglas Trumbull on the set of **Brainstorm**.

[2] A "spinner" rises above the city—Los Angeles in 2019—in **Blade Runner**.

that requires a very high suspension of disbelief, it may have been inappropriately applied to the project. People who see *The Hobbit* and say, 'Oh it looks too real' are complaining because they don't want it to look too real. They want it to look like a child's picture book. But if you apply the same, more realistic, tech to a movie like *Avatar*, it could be highly appropriate because *Avatar* is more like a theme park ride, where reality and futurism is completely appropriate."

Trumbull's UFOTOG project—a sci-fi short conceived to experiment with new immersive techniques and virtual sets—is designed to get an illusion on the screen that is, as he puts boldly, "almost indistinguishable from reality. I think we're just about there. So when you see a character on the screen you feel like you're almost in the room with that character. It's like a super virtual-reality experience."

2001: A Space Odyssey

Trumbull's journey on *2001: A Space Odyssey* began when director Kubrick and writer Arthur C. Clarke saw the Cinerama film *To The Moon and Beyond* at the 1964 New York World's Fair. Trumbull had contributed to the artwork and animations in the special venue film, imagery that had impressed Kubrick. When he moved to England to be part of *2001*, Trumbull—still in his early 20s—initially worked as an illustrator, but soon earned the trust of the perfectionist director to become one of the film's four effects supervisors.

"*2001* was really my film school," recalls Trumbull. "I was just intuitively comfortable with how to solve some of the problem's they were dealing with on set. I worked my way up the ladder during the production, from being a lowly animator doing HAL's readouts to being one of the effects supervisors. Kubrick really trusted my ingenuity and intuition about what would solve his problems."

One of the issues Trumbull helped solve for Kubrick was the blurring and strobing that would result from trying to move model spacecraft or stars across the screen. These were the days before computer-controlled motion-control cameras and computer graphics. "That problem has been faced by almost every filmmaker that has tried to put movies on a large screen," says Trumbull. "I realized we had to slow everything down, so everything in the movie moves at a very slow and majestic pace."

Another problematic shot Trumbull helped overcome was the depiction of astronaut Dr Dave Bowman (Keir Dullea) being pulled through a vortex of light, nebula-looking images, and starfields near Jupiter. Designated the "Star Gate" sequence, Trumbull suggested shooting moving footage made of back-lit colored artwork, chemicals, and high-contrast imagery with the shutter remaining open while the camera was also moved.

[1] A still from the "Star Gate" sequence. The slit-screen scan camera setup Trumbull adapted to make the sequence measured approximately 30 feet by 30 feet. It incorporated a movable slide with a slit cut into it between the artwork and the camera, which allowed Trumbull to expose parts of the artwork as the slide moved across.

[1]

[2] The spaceship Discovery One and an EVA pod. Shots of the model spacecraft were achieved using cameras placed on tracks that could have their moves mechanically repeated to enable star fields to be masked in behind them. Interior views of the ships were projected on rear-projection screens inside the windows.

[3] The "Star Gate" sequence from 2001 is perhaps one of Trumbull's most well-known accomplishments. Here he works on the various colored artworks.

This "slit-scan photography" technique required 60-second exposures and a specialized camera setup to capture the "slit" and the imagery behind it.

Despite the limitations of the day's technology, Trumbull says that Kubrick still succeeded in making the film he set out to make. It was also a defining moment for the visual effects supervisor's own career. "I just knew Kubrick was trying to make this immersive first-person trip for the audience, and ever since then I've been trying to do something better and find a way to dramatically increase the frame rate and quality, and keep the black levels very dark and increase color saturation and screen size. Basically every possible improvement we can make to the medium."

Close Encounters of the Third Kind

For Steven Spielberg's *Close Encounters of the Third Kind* (1977), Trumbull started a company with fellow effects supervisor Richard Yuricich, and set about advancing miniature construction and motion-control photography for the film's UFOs and mothership. The story would require smaller, fast-moving ships to appear and disappear in various shots, while the mothership was a major centerpiece.

Setting up in Marina Del Ray, Trumbull's company was a hive of activity on the film, comprising model makers, animators, matte painters, camera operators, optical compositors, and many more artists. The building housed a film-processing lab, optical printer, editing bays, and several stages that were used to shoot the models.

The mothership model was crafted out of fiberglass, measuring four foot high and five feet wide, and weighing 400lbs. The ship's most stunning features were its lights, which were made possible via long lengths of fiber optics, incandescent bulbs, and neon tubes wired into the model.

Integrating the UFOs and mothership into the scenes in the most realistic way possible was one of Spielberg's key requests to Trumbull and his crew—although it was a science-fiction story, the events in the film are of course portrayed as real-life occurrences. One approach involved mimicking the lens flares from the live photography in the miniature effects, which was achieved through optical compositing. Another technique was to shoot the models in heavy atmospheric smoke. For that, Trumbull had to ensure that filming could take place in dense, blacked-out smoke rooms that also kept the smoke levels consistent, as the models were filmed via motion control, in other words, only one frame every couple of seconds.

Another effects technique that helped ground the UFOs in the shots was the use of cloud tanks to produce atmospheric and cloud imagery—it was in the clouds that Spielberg had the alien spacecraft hiding. To create this effect, Trumbull's team built a 2,000-gallon glass tank that was filled with a combination of salt water and fresh water, layered between a plastic sheet. When the sheet was removed, the two waters remained separated. Paint could be injected into the tank and as the waters had two different densities, this would result in a cloud-like consistency. This would be captured on film and then optically composited into live-action plates; the final result much heralded and often copied in subsequent films.

[1] Clouds and lights appear near the house of Jillian Guiler (Melinda Dillon). This incredible effect was achieved using a cloud tank and optical compositing.

[1]

[2] The mothership at a site near Devils Tower, Wyoming. Fiber optic lights were a key component of the miniature ship's design.

[3] Douglas Trumbull on the set of **Close Encounters of the Third Kind**. The Academy of Motion Picture Arts and Sciences recognized the visual effects supervisor for his services to filmmaking with an honorary Academy Award in 2012.

Star Trek: The Motion Picture

When Paramount Pictures looked to revise their *Star Trek* franchise with Robert Wise's *Star Trek: The Motion Picture* (1979)—in which an alien V'Ger cloud threatens Earth—Trumbull was the first choice to complete the visual effects. At the time, he was consumed with the effects work on *Close Encounters of the Third Kind* and passed on the assignment. However, after difficulties with the company subsequently hired by Paramount to do the work, Trumbull came onto the production to complete partially finished effects shots, using existing models for some shots, and totally re-imagining others.

To help complete the effects in time, Trumbull (along with Richard Yuricich) re-assembled his *Close Encounters* team and also enlisted the help of John Dysktra's Apogee Productions. Dysktra had previously been instrumental in realizing the motion-control cameras for *Star Wars: Episode IV—A New Hope*, and had earlier collaborated with Trumbull on his film *Silent Running* in 1972.

Apogee tackled several sequences requiring miniatures, including the Epsilon IX, shots of the Enterprise's approach toward the V'Ger, and Klingon

[1] The Enterprise model and the motion-control camera setup, ready for shooting.

[1]

[2] A modelmaker works with a scale model of a travel pod.

[3] The view as Spock descends into the V'Ger.

K't'inga-class warships. Trumbull's company, EEG, delivered numerous other shots, such as interiors of the V'Ger and views of the Enterprise.

One of Trumbull's most memorable contributions to the film include Mr Spock's (Leonard Nimoy) space walk into the V'Ger as he seeks to contact the aliens. When it was deemed that the original wire work with Spock was unusable, Trumbull designed a new sequence and reshot some portions of the walk. Treating the performance of Nimoy more like a traditional model, the actor was mounted on a motion-control base in his spacesuit costume against a bluescreen, allowing for repeatable shots, and for epic V'Ger and space imagery to be composited behind him, as well as in front and into his helmet.

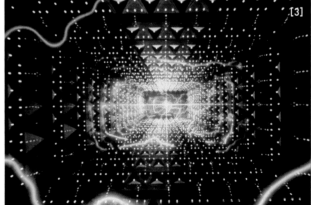

Blade Runner

Often cited—or appropriated—in futuristic films, the world of Ridley Scott's *Blade Runner* (1982) was yet another made possible by Trumbull and his team's effects artistry. A dystopian Los Angeles, circa 2019, with vast pyramids, giant display screens, advertisements, flying cars, and even rain came to life through many of the techniques Trumbull's team had perfected on *Close Encounters*—motion control, fiber optic lighting, smoke rooms, matte painting, and optical compositing. The noir-ish results, directly influenced by concepts from "visual futurist" Syd Mead, are some of the most memorable in science-fiction film history.

Blade Runner's opening sequence is a fly-through of Los Angeles, past fiery smoke stacks, with glimpses of the giant pyramids. The sequence became known as the "Hades Landscape," with Trumbull's Entertainment

Effects Group creating many of the buildings from flat miniature cut-outs that were acid-etched in brass to reveal small openings. Through these openings, artists placed hundreds of fiber optic and quartz lights. An arrangement of the miniatures was filmed via forced perspective through smoke, which added depth to the scene from all of the resulting light refraction. The explosions emanating from the stacks were actually practical fire elements—captured for a different film—projected onto screens in the miniature landscape. The pyramids appearing in this opening sequence were light boxes covered in photos that replicated the acid-etched artwork completed for miniature pyramids that had been built for close-up photography. Multiple elements shot for the sequence—including the flying "Spinner" vehicles—were then optically composited together.

[1] A classic scene from **Blade Runner** incorporating optical composites of miniature building photography, a 35mm projected display, and flying vehicles.

[1]

[2] A flying police vehicle, known as a Spinner, makes its way over the Tyrell Corporation Headquarters, which are in fact incredible acid-etched brass pyramid miniatures lit from below with fiber-optic lighting.

Various Spinner models were constructed for shooting, ranging from 1/12 to 1/4 scale (about one inch to 44 inches in length). Based on Syd Mead designs, the flying vehicles were cast in resin with plexiglass cockpits—the hero Spinner even featured miniature figurines of Deckard and Gaff, modeled and painted to look like Harrison Ford and Edward James Olmos. The Spinners also included the trademark fiber optic lights. Filmed in multiple passes with a motion-control camera, effects artists could adjust the amount of lens flare and police lighting in each shot.

The future Los Angeles of *Blade Runner* is besieged with large screens and advertising. In one particular scene, a blimp floats above a building in which replicants are hiding. Trumbull's crew built the "Bradbury Building Blimp" as a miniature, fitting it with fiber optic light bundles. To place displays on the blimp, as well as other buildings in the film, artists projected 35mm film imagery onto textured plastic. As the blimp would be seen through the atrium ceiling of the Bradbury Building—a real location in downtown Los Angeles—photographs there were captured and then glued to a giant sheet of glass. Skylight window holes were cut into the glass, allowing separate photography of the blimp to be composited through, along with smoke and other light sources.

15 > **Bill Westenhofer**

Bill Westenhofer has won two Academy Awards for achievement in visual effects, for *The Golden Compass* and *Life of Pi*, with a further Oscar nomination for his work on *The Chronicles of Narnia: The Lion, the Witch and the Wardrobe*. Those three films, which are just part of Westenhofer's substantial contributions to the industry, evidence the supervisor's strong affinity for creating realistic computer-generated characters.

Westenhofer developed a love for animation early on. "I was always drawing and painting as a kid," he says. "In fact, I made flipbooks in first grade to try to get people's milk money. I'd grab some paper and staple it together and make little flipbook animations."

At university, Westenhofer studied computer science and became engrossed in computer graphics. In 1994 he applied to work at Rhythm & Hues, a studio that in the early 1990s had pioneered CG animation and flying logos in TV commercials and then films. "I stuck my resume on the board at a conference and Rhythm & Hues granted me an interview on the day," he says. "I had a terrible demo reel—just stuff I'd written the software for and this crappy animation of an eagle flying over a mountain. But they gave me a shot."

"Right off the bat I did a commercial for Rice Krispies Treats," recalls Westenhofer. "It was live action and we had to put these thought bubbles in the air with floating Rice Krispies Treats inside." Westenhofer's first visual effects job might not have been glamorous, but it paved the way for work in the film industry, starting with *Batman Forever*, *Waterworld*, *Speed 2: Cruise Control*, and *Spawn*. There was then a relatively sudden elevation to visual effects supervisor for Rhythm & Hues on George Miller's *Babe: Pig in the City*, the follow-up to *Babe*, in which the studio's talking animal effects had first received attention and a visual effects Oscar.

Over the next decade and a half at Rhythm & Hues, Westenhofer would continue to have a close association with the creation of talking animals, which would evolve into fully CG-performing creatures and photoreal characters. His credits include the studio's visual effects supervisor on *Stuart Little*, *Along Came a Spider*, *Cats & Dogs*, *Men in Black II*, *Stuart Little 2*, *Elf*, and *The A-Team*.

Advancements led by work on *Narnia* and then *The Golden Compass*, fed directly into the photorealistic characters required for *Life of Pi*, a project Westenhofer considers was one he'd been "rehearsing for" ever since *Babe: Pig in the City*. "On *Life of Pi*," he says, "I sat the team down, and I said, 'we've done all these animals in the past, but this is the first time we don't have an animal that is going to sing or talk.' It was going to be a tiger that wouldn't give itself away for anything other than what we missed or didn't quite get. If we could pull it off, there would be scenes in there that we could fool our colleagues over."

Westenhofer suggests that the work on *Life of Pi*, and the films that came before it, were only possible with constant innovation on the part of his team of artists, even if sometimes the result did not look achievable at first. "As a visual effects supervisor," he says, "I describe this job sometimes as feeling like you've jumped off a cliff and you're counting on yourself to make a parachute before you land. One of the scariest parts is that I find it's my responsibility to project an air of confidence— even if that isn't genuinely the case—to a director who has so many other things to worry about. I'll take the trust I have in the people around me and project it forward, so the director can go about his or her business knowing we'll find a way to do it. The job can involve tough working conditions, long hours, and being away from your family, but we love doing this stuff and tackling problems."

[2] Richard Parker,
as featured in **Life of Pi**.
Westenhofer was lauded
for his work on this film with
the incredible photorealistic
portrayal of the tiger.

Babe: Pig in the City

Following the success of Chris Noonan's *Babe* (1995), director George Miller elected to follow the tale of the country pig with one involving more animals—a decision that would require more animatronic and digital effects to realize creature performances. *Babe: Pig in the City* (1998) would entail talking animal augmentation for the lead pig character, as well as other animals such as dogs, cats, and even chimpanzees.

"*Babe: Pig in the City* was really my first film as a supervisor," says Westenhofer, who admits on reflection that his practical photography skills at the time were not as advanced as his CG knowledge. But the opportunity was too good to miss. "I was going to be on set for the

[1] Babe and his new-found friends in the city would be brought to life with a combination of real animals, animatronic recreations by Neal Scanlan Studio, and digital visual effects work led by Rhythm & Hues, The Mill, and Animal Logic.

[1]

[2] With **Babe** and **Babe: Pig in the City**—along with other films, such as **Cats & Dogs**—Rhythm & Hues quickly developed a reputation as the go-to effects company for talking animals.

main shooting and really at the time I was an artist and a computer guy—not a photographer. So I was on the plane to Australia reading a cinematographer's guide. Andrew Lesnie was the DOP and he was just so great and I could approach him about anything."

"I knew how our software worked for talking animals and I knew the algorithms behind it," adds Westenhofer, "which meant I could make a call and know when a composite was going to work, even though I didn't have the more detailed experience."

At the time, the method used to make animals talk involved mostly a meticulous frame-by-frame approach. "We would build a 3D model of the animal head from lots of photographs we'd take," explains Westenhofer. "We also used the amazing animatronic creations made by Neal Scanlan Studio for the film as reference. There still isn't really a great way to cyberscan animals because they're not going to sit still for you!"

"The artists would then keep adjusting the model until it fit with what we could line up with the original photography," explains Westenhofer. "It was a fairly rough hand-animation process of hand tracking every frame to line up features. You'd do a hard track, which tracks the fixed positions of the eyes and the nose, and then you'd go in and do a hard track and deform—to line up frame by frame all the hard and soft tissue of the face."

Finally, a 3D CG process was applied. "We'd animate the things around the photography that would work with the geography," says Westenhofer. "We'd project every frame onto the rest of the model and that gets pulled around silly-putty style on a 3D model. The 3D shapes that weren't visible—tongues, teeth, mouth—were traditional 3D animation. Then there's a large part of the work that's paint fix-its as well."

The Chronicles of Narnia: The Lion, the Witch and the Wardrobe

With Andrew Adamson's *The Chronicles of Narnia: The Lion, the Witch and the Wardrobe* (2005), Westenhofer needed to deliver both a hero talking animal in the lion Aslan (voiced by Liam Neeson) and a bevy of other mythological creatures, including gryphons, centaurs, minotaurs, and fauns.

For Aslan, the visual effects supervisor identified early on that lion reference would be key. That came from a day at animal training facility, Gentle Jungle, in Frazier Park, California. Here, a lion could be observed, as well as a cheetah, leopard, eagle, bear, and wolves—creatures that Rhythm & Hues would end up replicating for the film's final battle.

"From that reference we noted that weight is really important," says Westenhofer. "It really defines the leap from a fully-animated film to reality. Human beings in general are really good at looking at something that's fake—the hard part is identifying what things to do to

make it look real. You put the CG animal down as an animation and weigh it up against the photography and see what works and what doesn't. We take hero angles and line up the digital model and we just literally wipe back and forth to see what's matching."

Aslan would require a step-up in the way Rhythm & Hues produced realistic fur—the lion's groom would ultimately combine 15 different hair types just in the mane. "When you're at a facility," details Westenhofer, "the only time you're going to get all the time to put the tools together is at the beginning of a project. I looked at where all our hair tools were, and the hair tools for Aslan came about on *Cats & Dogs*. That was really the first time we did real 3D hair primitives and lighting, and I knew we had to really make a lot of improvements."

What also helped sell the digital animals—especially Aslan—as "real" in the scenes, was introducing the appearance of wind in the fur, partly to match the

[1] The centaur Oreius (Patrick Kake). Depending on the kind of shot that was required, centaurs would be achieved by augmenting real photography of an actor riding a horse; via motion capture of horse and rider; or by having an actor walk on a platform in greenscreen stockings and then matchmoving that performance to a computer-generated horse body.

[1]

[2] Aslan—a completely CG creation. Facial animation was critical in realizing the stately lion. Although Liam Neeson would ultimately be cast as Aslan's voice, Rhythm & Hues originally referenced the powerful performance of Gregory Peck's character Atticus Finch from **To Kill a Mockingbird** so that the Aslan CG rig could replicate similar expressions.

strong winds present while filming on location in New Zealand. Rhythm & Hues actually simulated two kinds of wind—"dynamic wind" that would replicate a strong breeze pushing hair around, and "pelt wind" to show the movement of wispy hair edges in a slighter breeze.

Westenhofer also considers the gryphons (with their elaborate wings and feathers) and the centaurs (a mix of human and of horse) as some of the more challenging creations required for *The Lion, the Witch and the Wardrobe*. Many shots of the centaurs relied on motion capture of a horse with its rider that Rhythm & Hues combined to sell the right movement. For the final battle, these—and other animal animations—were fed into crowd simulation software known as "Massive," to show up to 30,000 creatures on screen at the same time. In total, Rhythm & Hues built 67 unique characters for

the first Narnia tale, a task that Westenhofer knew would require an upfront investment in its visual effects tools. The film ultimately made full use of a robust technical pipeline that Rhythm & Hues had been employing for some time—a toolset known as "Voodoo."

The studio had built Voodoo as a proprietary system for rigging and animating its characters, as well as enabling scenes to be camera tracked and match moved. On *Narnia*, the system was widely extended to handle more fur simulation, crowds, and lighting.

"With so many creatures outdoors," notes Westenhofer, "we really had to prove our ability to efficiently rig and animate all these characters and do things like take world maps projected on a sphere and use that to light the character. It was a step toward more realism."

The Golden Compass

Westenhofer's *Narnia* experience informed his next major project—Chris Weitz's *The Golden Compass* (2007)—for which he oversaw Rhythm & Hues' creation of many of the film's dæmons. These are, in the story, animal counterparts to a person's being, ranging from ferrets to dogs to cats to monkeys, and more.

"We did about 20 different animals," says Westenhofer. "I think the most interesting aspect of the production was the close integration with animals on people. Things like a cat going through a girl's hair, which meant we had to build digital hair, or the cat leaping up into her arms,

which had to look convincing." To help with that integration, actors often held material representations of their dæmons, essentially greenscreen- or bluescreen-covered bean bags that would be replaced with CG animals by the visual effects artists. Or similar animal representations might be swung into view on a pole or fishing line.

"When an actor holds something, there can be an imperfection in how they do it, like a slip for example," explains Westenhofer. "Having those imperfections is almost critical, because you can take advantage of

[1] For Mrs. Coulter's Golden Monkey dæmon, Westenhofer's effects team crafted a digital "hairnet" to control its fur and ensure it remained stiff.

[1]

[2] Lord Asriel (Daniel Craig) and his dæmon Stelmaria, a CG snow leopard.

them and come up with a justification that makes it look like there's a degree of inter-relationship that had to be dropped together. It gives a complexity that makes it feel like an onject is really there."

The dæmons also had to match their human's personality. The character of Mrs. Coulter (Nicole Kidman) has dark traits, for example, so Rhythm & Hues ensured that her Golden Monkey dæmon exhibited similar behaviors. Effects artists based its design on a mix between capuchin, spider, and three types of tamarind monkey.

A further challenge with the dæmons was that some of the animals had not yet settled into their final form, so would transform from one creature into another.

For example, Pantalaimon ("Pan"), the soul creature behind lead character Lyra Belacqua (Dakota Blue Richards), shape-shifts at one point between a mouse and a cat. These shots, notes Westenhofer, incorporated geometry changes in animation and specific behavior, such as a head or body shake as the transformation occurs. When a person dies in the story, its dæmon passes away in a waft of dust—an effect that was achieved using fluid-simulation software.

Life of Pi

Ang Lee's *Life of Pi* (2012) struck a chord with audiences, who were enthralled by the stunningly photorealistic animals in a film that also contained fantastical elements. Much of the film takes place in a lifeboat in the middle of the ocean. Westenhofer determined that real wildlife reference would be crucial in bringing the central tiger character, Richard Parker, to life. "I took a risk and we put some real tigers on the boat," he says. "Even though I knew there would be a limit to what we could really do with them, having them there meant I'd have eight weeks of unlimited access to get as much reference as we possibly could."

Significant advancements in rendering fur, including the sub-surface scattering of light through the fur and producing convincing wet fur when Richard Parker jumps into the ocean, were realized by Rhythm & Hues on the film. Again, this detail originated from the live-action reference.

"Without the reference I wouldn't think of half the things we put in there," adds Westenhofer. "If you sit an animator down and say 'give me a tiger just sitting there,' we as humans are so used to idealizing things and the way we interpret the world we just miss the real details if we're not studying the detail. We use motion capture more these days, but we've never really found a good way to mocap animals. Mocap is really great, but you need to get that last little thing—tiny vibrations when you stop, and other little things. If they're not there, then there's an artificiality that you're always going to fight."

To ensure a realistic swell was captured for the ocean scenes, filming occurred in a 75 x 30 meter tank surrounded by bluescreen. Pistons sucked in water and generated the required wave patterns, with special "tetrapod" wave breaks placed into the tank to reduce wave bounce-back on the lifeboat.

For the visual effects crew, the tank would provide definitive wave motion to base their boat performance on, but it would also prove troublesome to matchmove CG water and sky extensions, and place digital animals into the craft. Says Westenhofer: "There were a couple

[1] A whale breeches the water through a gathering of phosphorescent plankton—one of many visual effects overseen by Westenhofer for the film.

[1]

[2] Richard Parker and Pi (Suraj Sharma) face the wide ocean. Real photography of a lifeboat filmed in a water tank surrounded by bluescreen was the starting point for Rhythm & Hues' visual effects work. Richard Parker's face relied on the combination of a CG muscle rig with blend shapes that could be pushed and pulled by the animators.

[3] The bluescreen setup showing the real lifeboat floating in a tank.

of days on the tank when we're 3D (the film was shot in stereo) and we've got to blend the tank water into a digital surface—just tracking something on a flat surface is hard enough. You have to go with your gut at times and say 'I know the people I'm working with can do this.' And they did."

On the tank set, Westenhofer also engaged animation supervisor Erik de Boer to stand in for the CG tiger, including for a scene where thousands of flying fish enter the boat. Here, Pi pushes a grappling hook at Richard Parker who grabs it with his mouth. Erik de Boer would act out the tussle with the hook to ensure that it felt like Pi was really fighting with the tiger.

Richard Parker was, of course, only one of the challenges encountered by Westenhofer and the visual effects crew. They also had to imagine a zebra, cheetah, and orangutan on the boat, as well as a leaping whale and an island inhabited by thousands of meerkats.

Westenhofer credits his team with taking finished shots to the next level, even after Ang Lee had signed off on them. "It's a tough sell to producers," he admits,

"but you almost have to say 'I'm going to go get this shot finaled by the director and as soon as that happens I'm going to give myself another week to work on the fine stuff that you don't want to commit to until the shot's not going to change any more.' That was something we did on *Life of Pi*, which I thought was essential to the fidelity of the animation."

16 > Edson Williams

[1]

Edson Williams once had a job in visual effects that he was not allowed to talk about. As a specialist in digital cosmetic "beauty" fixes, his work was often invisible and intended to stay that way. But Williams was soon able to apply his skills to carry out de-aging, face, and body replacement effects in films such as _X-Men: The Last Stand_, _The Curious Case of Benjamin Button_, _The Social Network_, and the _Captain America_ movies—crucial effects that helped the directors tell critical story points. Williams and his company, Lola Visual Effects, are now sought after for exactly these sorts of shots.

Williams' first visual effects assignment was on Roland Emmerich's _Stargate_ (1994). "I was teaching a Photoshop and Alias Power Animator class at Brooks Institute of Photography in Santa Barbara, California," he says. "At the time, Wavefront Technologies, a 3D software company, was also based in Santa Barbara, and I hung out with some of their programmers. One afternoon, a programmer from Wavefront called and asked if I could help him with a side project he was recently awarded. He needed someone to composite the 3D-rendered rings that transported humans to other worlds. I answered yes, and my career grew from there."

Before moving into beauty and face replacement work, Williams contributed to traditional visual effects films such as _Volcano_, where he helped create lava, and _Titanic_, crafting the iceberg that sinks the ship. "It was music videos that pushed me to create a company specializing in digital cosmetics," relates Williams. "It struck me as odd that a singer in a $100,000 music video would get their eye bags and pimples removed, but the leading actress in a $100-million dollar movie was left untouched. One day we received a call from a studio that wanted to add a six-pack to its aging action star. It was only one shot, but that single six-pack ab shot was the straw that broke the camel's back and we started Lola about three months later."

Audiences were amazed at seeing a young Patrick Stewart and Ian McKellen on the screen in the _X-Men: The Last Stand_, a feat Williams and Lola bettered by rejuvenating Brad Pitt and Cate Blanchett for _The Curious Case of Benjamin Button_. Then in _The Social Network_, many viewers were convinced that twins had

played the role of Cameron and Tyler Winklevoss—but again it was Lola trickery that had achieved that effect. Perhaps the most stunning transformations Lola has worked on, however, came with "Skinny Steve" and "Old Peggy" in the _Captain America_ films.

While Williams and Lola still contribute work other than beauty fixes or face and body replacements to many feature films, their mandate continues to be invisible effects. "I believe visual effects in modern filmmaking has two distinct paths; in your face, and hidden from view," he says. "A dinosaur or angry robot chasing the actors through the scene is always exciting, but so much of a good movie is subtle effects that help a director tell an emotional story. The love scene may not have the same impact if the stars have deep eye bags, rough skin, and puffy cheeks. My specialty is invisible cosmetic effects—if you leave the theater thinking your favorite actor has perfect skin and no body fat, then I did my job."

[1] Edson Williams.

[2] Lola Visual Effects shrunk actor Chris Evans in size and stature before he became the superhero in **Captain America: The First Avenger**.

[3] The character became known as "Skinny Steve," whose gaunt appearance involved mostly 2D-scaling effects on Evans' head and body, but also made use of body doubles.

X-Men: The Last Stand

"Lola Visual Effects has been involved in several firsts for feature films," notes Williams, "and *X-Men: The Last Stand* (2006) is a great example." Here, director Brett Ratner called on the studio to complete visual effects for a flashback scene involving the characters of Magneto (Ian McKellen) and Charles Xavier (Patrick Stewart). Lola would need to "youthen" the actors, to make them appear 25 years younger. This was an effect that might have traditionally been done with makeup, but the filmmakers—including overall supervisor John Bruno— trusted Lola and Williams to do this digitally, based on their successful history of film beauty work.

"Prior to *X-Men* we had worked on several movies where we did slight age reductions, but nothing compared to the scope of this project," says Williams. "The producers gave us a scene from a previous movie to test how far we could push our technology. We began by viewing photos of Ian and Patrick when they were young men. Both actors have been on stage and in the movies for their entire adult lives—this presented a double-edged sword, as there were many reference photos to choose from, but the audience would also know if we didn't nail it exactly."

"Our initial testing dropped us right in the middle of 'The Uncanny Valley,'" notes Williams, referring to the studied phenomenon that when human features look almost, but not exactly correct, it causes a response of discomfort in the viewer. "Something in our test was not right, we made the actors look like they had bad plastic surgery. We had to rethink the process, and break it down into individual steps like a surgeon would—digital derm abrasion, nose jobs, and finally a face lift using deformation tools."

[1] Patrick Stewart (foreground left) and Ian McKellen (foreground right) as they appear in the present day in **X-Men: The Last Stand**. For a flashback sequence, Williams oversaw complicated compositing techniques to make the actors appear younger.

[2] A shot revealing the rejuvenating effects orchestrated by Lola Visual Effects, which took account of consultations with plastic surgeons on how facial features change with age.

In researching human faces, Williams consulted with plastic surgeons and discovered that noses and ears continue to grow as a person ages, so in general, McKellen and Stewart's features were removed, downsized ten percent, and re-tracked onto their faces. Several "digital skin graft" methods were also used in compositing software to soften skin details, provide color correction, and 3D track features, while also closely matching the lighting from the original plates. Another incredible aspect of the shots was that the actors did not wear any special makeup, hair coloring, or tracking markers for Lola to work with—that was all achieved in postproduction.

Williams and five other artists worked on the first youthening shot of Stewart and McKellen for six weeks before they felt confident enough to show a test composite to the film studio. "About 2,000 hours of labor produced a single rough temp, 124 frames long," states Williams. "By the end of the project, we had reduced the labor down to around 300 hours per shot."

The Curious Case of Benjamin Button

David Fincher's *The Curious Case of Benjamin Button* (2008) tells the story of a man, played by Brad Pitt, who ages in reverse. During the film, Pitt therefore had to be shown at various ages—as an old man, his current age, and his younger self. It was this young Benjamin that Lola and Williams orchestrated.

"Digital Domain did the first half of the movie using a fully synthetic CG head," explains Williams. "They drove the animation using facial performance capture of Brad Pitt wearing tracking dots on his face. Their technique worked amazingly well until Benjamin became a grown man, that's when my team at Lola took over."

"David Fincher wanted to maintain all the subtle performances of Brad Pitt, and our work on *X-Men: The Last Stand* gave Mr. Fincher the confidence we could refine the technique to his satisfaction," adds Williams. "Lola knew how to de-age an actor, but our process in *X-Men* also stripped away some of the life of the characters. Maintaining all the subtleties of the human face proved incredibly challenging."

As they had done on *X-Men: The Last Stand*, Williams' team at Lola took original footage of Pitt, and also Cate Blanchett who plays Button's childhood friend, Daisy Fullerm. These were passed through the company's

[1] Brad Pitt and Cate Blanchett in **The Curious Case of Benjamin Button**. Lola Visual Effects used de-aging compositing techniques to "adjust" the facial features of each of the performers.

[1]

[2] The de-aging effects overseen by Williams were necessary to show the changing ages in Pitt and Blanchett's characters.

digital skin-grafting process. In particular, several scenes at Benjamin's home in New Orleans and at Daisy's ballet studio made use of the de-aging effects. Importantly, although the effects artists had many techniques for completing the work, the answer was not a simple, "one-touch" approach—it involved hours of meticulous artistry.

Once again, the important aspect of the shots was to preserve whatever lighting and performance had been in the original plate. "I would sit in our

theater for several hours a day looking at split screens with our latest comps on the right, and the originals on the left," says Williams. "It was the best way we had to find subtle changes, like a brow furrowing slightly less or a lost twitch in the corner of the mouth. David Fincher's ability to see the smallest element of a performance forced Lola to a new level of precision, and all the projects we have done since have greatly benefited from his involvement."

The Social Network

David Fincher would again request the help of Williams and Lola on his exploration of the Facebook story in *The Social Network* (2010). In the film, Facebook founder Mark Zuckerberg (Jesse Eisenberg) is shown in the middle of depositions relating to a number of lawsuits against him. One is pursued by fellow Harvard upperclassmen and twins Cameron and Tyler Winklevoss and their business partner Divya Narendra.

The Winklevoss twins were played by the same actor—Armie Hammer—with Lola helping to make Cameron and Tyler appear on the screen together in a seamless fashion.

"Most of the shots," notes Williams, "could be done using split screens where essentially the same actor performs the scene twice, once for each character. The two separate performances are joined together later, giving the illusion of identical twins acting with each other. But the split-screen approach has limitations, for instance, how do you have a single actor play two people rowing a boat down a river? One option would be to have

[1] Max Minghella and Armie Hammer in **The Social Network**. Hammer played both Tyler and Cameron Winklevoss in the film, thanks to the visual efforts of Lola VFX.

[2] Edson Williams demonstrates a custom rig made up of 12 computer-controlled lights used to capture facial imagery. The rig was first utilized on **The Social Network**.

the hero actor row a boat with a body double playing the second rower, then later in post, replace the body-double's face with a computer-generated face. But creating a fully synthetic face requires massive computer rendering power and a large specialized team of artists including 3D modelers, riggers, 3D lighters, animators, texture artists, and compositors."

However, Lola's entire 3D department consisted of one artist, so they looked for what Williams describes as a "more elegant solution." "Fortunately, David Fincher had a radical idea," recalls Williams. "Instead of creating a CG replica of Armie Hammer, he suggested re-shooting Armie's actual performance, projecting it onto 3D geometry, and tracking the combined element onto a body-double's face. The advantage to this new technique was our ability to use real skin, real eyes, a real mouth, and maintain all the original subtle performance of Hammer."

To enable that technique, Lola built a custom rig that comprised of 12 computer-controlled lights and four RED EPIC cameras. Armie performed Winklevoss lines in the rig, while referencing a correct eyeline from a screen in front of him that had an animated dot to follow. "The lights were controlled by a DMX panel, similar to what you would find at a rock concert," says Williams. "We analyzed the light that was in the scene and on the body-double's face, then we recreated it using the DMX programmable controller. When Armie was in the Lola rig, he did not move his head through the lighting—we virtually moved the lights around him."

During filming of the principal photography, Hammer would play opposite actor Josh Pence, who wore tracking dots on his face while playing the other twin. Oftentimes Pence also wore a hat or headband to provide a clean line for Lola to then graft the appropriate Winklevoss face onto the actor. That face came from the captured Hammer performance—projection mapped onto a digital version of the actor's head.

One major success of the shots, points out Williams, is that they were able to be done by a relatively small company. Lola has less than 40 employees. "This small size forces us to be creative in our approach to visual effects," he says. "The shots worked incredibly well, and our face-projection technique has been adopted by the visual-effects industry."

Captain America: The First Avenger and The Winter Soldier

With Joe Johnston's *Captain America: The First Avenger* (2011), Williams and Lola expanded upon their proven facial performance and rejuvenating effects to reveal the scrawny character of Steve Rogers (Chris Evans) before he becomes the bulked-up superhero Captain America. The resulting effect became known as "Skinny Steve."

The work involved two main approaches. One saw the use of a body double, with stage actor Leander Deeny standing in for Evans on set. Lola would then utilize the face-projection techniques it had developed on *The Social Network* to track a shrunk-down version of Evans' head onto Deeny's body. The second, and most common, approach was to carry out 2D scaling effects on Evans' face and body itself, implementing the appropriate gaunt look. Since his new smaller stature would reveal elements behind him, Lola would have to repair backgrounds behind Evans, too.

For the follow-up to *The First Avenger*—the Anthony and Joe Russo-directed film *The Winter Soldier* (2014)—Lola returned to create effects for a scene in which

Rogers visits his former love interest, Peggy Carter (Hayley Atwell), who is now around 90-years old and living in a nursing home. After much experimentation, "Old Peggy" would ultimately be realized by Lola by re-applying the skin of an elderly lady onto Atwell's performance.

"The studio and the directors stressed that it was critical for Hayley's emotions and performance to come through," says Williams. "We planned on tackling the challenge of aging Peggy using face projections. We shot Hayley on set with a gray wig and a few tracking dots on her face, but no other age makeup was used at this stage. The next step was to do a test shoot of Hayley wearing old age prosthetic appliances with makeup on top. The test was less than acceptable, so we had a larger challenge than we anticipated."

Williams notes that the initial appliances were thick, took hours to apply, and had the effect of dampening Hayley's underlying performance. "We knew we needed to do additional testing, but it was a taxing process, and

[1] Original photography of actress Haley Atwell playing Peggy Carter.

[2] A final shot of "Old Peggy" by Lola Visual Effects, made possible by digitally grafting skin from an elderly lady onto Atwell's performance.

we had limited time with Hayley Atwell. So we hired a model matching Hayley's age to continue to refine the old-age makeup. Each iteration got better and better, as the appliances continued to get thinner. The painted skin also continued to improve greatly. We decided to hire an elderly woman to match Hayley's dialog and performance. Our intention was to use this as a reference for the practical makeup team."

After seeing the footage of the older actress, Williams recognized how much more convincing real skin looked and how it resulted in the performance being uninhibited. "So I came up with a radical idea," he says. "What if we took makeup out of the equation altogether? What if we just stole actual skin from the elderly lady and projected it onto Hayley's face? No bulky appliances, no makeup, no four hours in a makeup chair. This idea of a skin transfer sounded crazy at first, but as fate would have it, about six months earlier, Lola had developed a skin-grafting technique to remove a beard from an actor—it was for a continuity fix. A few days later we showed a

test to the studio and said, 'We have a Hail Mary pass for you.' The studio loved it."

The final look relied on several refinements and digitally grafting parts from four different elderly ladies. "We also continued to allow more and more of Hayley's original skin to come through," says Williams. "We tried to use just the shadows and creases of the old projected face, and that allowed Hayley's performance to come through. We had just created an old-age sequence without practical makeup—these were the hardest shots I have ever worked on, and the most satisfying."

[2]

Glossary >

Animatic—a rough version of a sequence in the form of edited-together storyboards or other visual elements.

Animatronic—a practical puppet that typically incorporates robotics or electronics for lifelike animation and movement.

Anamorphic—a system of filming where a widescreen picture is acquired on non-widescreen film by squeezing the image captured vertically, and then projecting that image by stretching it back into the correct aspect ratio.

Bluescreen/greenscreen—a blue or green backing that can be set up behind moving actors or objects, allowing for easy isolation of that blue or green color in order to composite the actor or objects against a separately filmed or generated background.

CGI—computer generated imagery, also known as "CG" or "3D."

Cloud tank—a glass tank that is often filled with different liquids, colors, and materials that, when filmed, provides the illusion of clouds or other atmospheric effects.

Compositing—combining two or more images together to form one final image. It is a technique once carried out via an optical printer with real film, but is now done using digital techniques.

Computer simulation—the process of using software to generate real-world phenomena, such as simulations of water, fire, clouds, dust, fur, and so on.

Cyberscan—the scanning of a person or object using a laser (or similar) to digitize their dimensions and likeness in order to create an equivalent CG model.

DOP—director of photography, often also known as the cinematographer.

Forced perspective—a technique for filming characters or objects by placing them closer or further away from the camera lens and therefore making them appear bigger or larger in the frame.

Fps—frames per second, also referred to as "frame rate." The number of consecutive frames generated in a second of filming.

Grading—also known as color correction, color grading, or color timing, this is the process of digitally or photochemically adjusting the light values of an image, often for certain effects and commonly to match pieces of footage shot or created at different times.

Key-frame animation—the process of drawing or defining each frame in the movement of a character or object that is being animated.

LIDAR—an acronym for Light Detection and Ranging, a system that uses a laser to measure distance from an object via reflected light, the results of which can help produce 3D spatial information about the areas measured.

Light meter—an instrument that is able to measure the intensity of light, often used on set to help determine the correct exposure in photography.

Matchmoving—the process of tracking the motion of an object or the camera in a scene, as well as changes in size, scale, angle, and orientation, typically to allow CG elements to be inserted seamlessly.

Matte painting—a painted version of a scene, often a landscape or vista. Prior to the advent of CGI, matte paintings were commonly done on glass with "hold out" areas into which live action photography could be projected or composited.

Miniature—a term sometimes used interchangeably with "model," miniatures are scaled representations of almost anything that can be imagined such as buildings, characters, vehicles, and landscapes.

Motion blur—the appearance of streaking on a moving image, caused in film cameras by the movement of the subject while a frame is being recorded.

Motion capture—the process of recording movements in space, usually with infrared cameras and special tracking markers, and translating that movement digitally to another character, creature, or even a virtual camera. Often shortened to "mocap" and sometimes referred to as performance capture.

Motion-control camera—a camera that is positioned on a motorized and computerized rig that can be programmed so camera movements are repeatable. The process allows multiple layers to be produced that can be composited together to form a final shot.

Optical printer—a device that enables optical compositing by positioning multiple projectors so that several layers of film with different elements on them can be projected onto a new piece of film.

Previsualization—often shortened to "previs." The process of using rough, low-resolution CG models and environments to plan filmed sequences, particularly ones that might involve complex stunts, or special and visual effects.

Principal photography—in feature film production, the stage of filming involving the main acquisition of actor performances, usually coming after pre-production and before post-production.

Prosthetic makeup—a special effects makeup technique involving the sculpting or casting of prosthetic appliances for enhanced practical facial or body makeup effects.

Pyro—short for pyrotechnics. Includes the special effects techniques of explosions and fire elements.

Rendering—the process of generating a final image in computer graphics by calculating the combination of light and textures on a 2D or 3D image.

Rigging—adding in joints and structure to CG models, such as an under-skeleton to a digital creature.

Rigid-body simulation—a computer simulation involving an element that is a solid surface, such as a vehicle or building.

Rotoscoping—the process of tracing over footage, often frame by frame, to isolate a particular section of it for the purpose of adding imagery to that footage or to replicate a moving performance in the scene.

Split screen—an effects technique where two or more shots are combined into one shot, often by acquiring non-overlapping images, such as performances from the same actor in two different sections of the screen.

Stereo in film, the capturing and projection of two images that create the impression of depth when viewed together.

Stop motion—an animation technique involving moving an object and a camera one frame at a time to provide the illusion of continuous movement once the footage is played back at normal speed.

Texture mapping—the process of adding detail or graphics to the surface of a CG model.

Virtual production—the extrapolation of traditional on-set filming techniques to computer graphics and visual effects techniques, including previsualization, on-set performance capture, and virtual camera movement.

Index >

Picture Credits

Front cover image: **Avatar** courtesy of Twentieth Century-Fox Film Corporation/The Kobal Collection; Back cover images: **Pirates of the Caribbean: Dead Man's Chest** courtesy of Walt Disney/The Kobal Collection; **Life of Pi** courtesy of Fox 2000 Pictures/Dune Entertainment/Ingenious Media/Haishang Films/The Kobal Collection; **The Hobbit: An Unexpected Journey** courtesy of New Line Cinema/The Kobal Collection; **Terminator 2: Judgment Day** courtesy of Carolco/The Kobal Collection; **Hugo** courtesy GK Films/The Kobal Collection; Inside back cover images: **Pirates of the Caribbean: Curse of the Black Pearl** courtesy of Walt Disney/The Kobal Collection; **Green Lantern** courtesy of Warner Bros./DC Entertainment/The Kobal Collection; **Captain America: The First Avenger** courtesy of Marvel/Paramount/The Kobal Collection; p1 **Avatar** courtesy of Twentieth Century-Fox Film Corporation/The Kobal Collection; p2–3 **The Hobbit: An Unexpected Journey** courtesy of New Line Cinema/The Kobal Collection; p4–5 **The Abyss** courtesy of 20th Century Fox/The Kobal Collection; **The Dark Knight** courtesy of Warner Bros/DC Comics/The Kobal Collection; **Ghostbusters** courtesy of Columbia/The Kobal Collection; **Transformers** courtesy of Dreamworks/The Kobal Collection; **The Dark Knight Rises** courtesy of Warner Bros. Pictures/The Kobal Collection; **10,000 Years BC** courtesy of Warner Bros. Pictures/The Kobal Collection; **Batman Begins** courtesy of Warner Bros./D.C. Comics/The Kobal Collection/James, David; **Star Wars: Episode I—The Phantom Menace** courtesy of LucasFilm/The Kobal Collection; **Titanic** courtesy of 20th Century Fox/Paramount/The Kobal Collection; **The Lord of the Rings: The Return of the King** courtesy of New Line Cinema/The Kobal Collection; **Jurassic Park** courtesy of Amblin/Universal/The Kobal Collection; **Terminator 2: Judgment Day** courtesy of Carolco/The Kobal Collection; **Starship Troopers** courtesy of Columbia Tristar/The Kobal Collection; **Blade Runner** courtesy of Ladd Company/Warner Bros/The Kobal Collection; **Life of Pi** courtesy of Fox 2000 Pictures/Dune Entertainment/Ingenious Media/Haishang Films/The Kobal Collection; **Captain America: The First Avenger** courtesy of Marvel/Paramount/The Kobal Collection; p6 **Avatar** courtesy of Twentieth Century-Fox Film Corporation/The Kobal Collection; p9 Photo by Jim Spellman/WireImage; p10 **Star Wars: Episode IV—A New Hope** courtesy of LucasFilm/20th Century Fox/The Kobal Collection; p11 **Life of Pi** courtesy of Fox 2000 Pictures/Dune Entertainment/Ingenious Media/Haishang Films/The Kobal Collection; p12 Courtesy of Richard Edlund; p13 **X-Men: The Last Stand** courtesy of 20th Century Fox/The Kobal Collection; p14 **Ghostbusters** courtesy of Columbia/The Kobal Collection; p15 Courtesy of Richard Edlund; p16 **The Abyss** Photo © AF archive/Alamy; p17 (2) **The Abyss** courtesy of 20th Century Fox/The Kobal Collection; p17 (3) **The Abyss** courtesy of 20th Century Fox/The Kobal Collection; p18 **True Lies** Photo © Douglas Kirkland/Corbis; p19 **True Lies** courtesy of Lightstorm Entertainment/The Kobal Collection/Rosenthal, Zade; p20 **X-Men: The Last Stand** courtesy of 20th Century Fox/The Kobal Collection; p21 **X-Men: The Last Stand** courtesy of 20th Century Fox/The Kobal Collection; p22 Photo by Dave M. Benett/WireImage; p23 Courtesy of Chris Corbould OBE; p24 **GoldenEye** courtesy of Danjaq/EON/UA/The Kobal Collection; p25 **GoldenEye** courtesy of Danjaq/EON/UA/The Kobal Collection; p26–27 **Die Another Day** courtesy of MGM/EON/The Kobal Collection/Maidment, Jay; p28 **The Dark Knight** courtesy of Warner Bros/DC Comics/The Kobal Collection; p29 **Batman Begins** courtesy of Warner Bros/DC Comics/The Kobal Collection/James, David; p30–31 **Inception** courtesy of Warner Bros/The Kobal Collection; p32 **Skyfall** courtesy of Danjaq/EON Productions/The Kobal Collection; p33 **Skyfall** courtesy of Danjaq/EON Productions/The Kobal Collection; p34 Courtesy of Richard Edlund/Photograph by Owen Roisman, ASC; p35 **Star Wars: Episode V—The Empire Strikes Back** courtesy of LucasFilm/20th Century Fox/The Kobal Collection; p36 **Star Wars: Episode IV—A New Hope** courtesy of LucasFilm/20th Century Fox/The Kobal Collection; p37 **Star Wars: Episode IV—A New Hope** courtesy of LucasFilm/20th Century Fox/The Kobal Collection; p38 **Raiders of the Lost Ark** courtesy of LucasFilm Ltd./Paramount/The Kobal Collection; p39 (2) **Raiders of the Lost Ark** courtesy of LucasFilm Ltd./Paramount/The Kobal Collection; p39 (3) **Raiders of the Lost Ark** courtesy of LucasFilm Ltd./Paramount/The Kobal Collection; p40 **Ghostbusters** courtesy of Columbia/The Kobal Collection; p41 **Ghostbusters** courtesy of Columbia/The Kobal Collection; p42 **Multiplicity** courtesy of Columbia/The Kobal Collection; p43 **Multiplicity** courtesy of Columbia/The Kobal Collection; p44 Photo © Scott Kirkland/Retna Ltd./Corbis; p45 **Transformers** courtesy of Dreamworks/The Kobal Collection; p46 **Back to the Future II** courtesy of Amblin/Universal/The Kobal Collection; p47 **Back to the Future** courtesy of Amblin/Universal/The Kobal Collection; p48 courtesy of 20th Century Fox/Dreamworks/The Kobal Collection/ILM (Industrial Light & Magic); p49 **Minority Report** courtesy of 20th Century Fox/Dreamworks/The Kobal Collection; p50 **Transformers** courtesy of Dreamworks/The Kobal Collection; p51 **Transformers** courtesy of Dreamworks/The Kobal Collection; p52 **Transformers: Age of Extinction** courtesy of Paramount Pictures/Hasbro/Di Bonaventura Pictures/The Kobal Collection; p53 **Transformers: Age of Extinction** courtesy of Paramount Pictures/Hasbro/Di Bonaventura Pictures/The Kobal Collection; p54 **World War Z** courtesy of Paramount Pictures/The Kobal Collection; p55 **World War Z** courtesy of Paramount Pictures/The Kobal Collection; p56: Photo by Maury Phillips/Getty Images for VES; p57 **Interstellar** courtesy of Paramount/Warner Brothers/The Kobal Collection; p58 **Pitch Black** courtesy of Gramercy Pictures/The Kobal Collection/Barnes, Sean; p59 **Pitch Black** courtesy of Gramercy Pictures/The Kobal Collection/Barnes, Sean; p60 **Batman Begins** courtesy of Warner Bros./D.C. Comics/The Kobal Collection/James, David; p61 **Batman Begins** courtesy of Warner Bros./D.C. Comics/The Kobal Collection/James, David; p62 **The Dark Knight** courtesy of Warner Bros./D.C. Comics/The Kobal Collection; p63 **The Dark Knight Rises** courtesy of Warner Bros. Pictures/The Kobal Collection; p64 **Inception** courtesy of Warner Bros./The Kobal Collection; p65 **Inception** courtesy of Warner Bros./The Kobal Collection; p66 Courtesy of Karen Goulekas/Photograph by Jerry Hall; p67 **The Fifth Element** courtesy of Columbia/Tri-Star/The Kobal Collection; p68 **Godzilla** courtesy of Columbia Tri-Star/The Kobal Collection/Centropolis Effects; p69 **Godzilla** courtesy of Columbia Tri-Star/The Kobal Collection; p70 **The Day After Tomorrow** courtesy of 20th Century Fox/The Kobal Collection; p71 **The Day After Tomorrow** courtesy of 20th Century Fox/The Kobal Collection; p72 **10,000 Years BC** courtesy of Warner Bros. Pictures/The Kobal Collection; p73 **10,000 Years BC** courtesy of Warner Bros. Pictures/The Kobal Collection; p74 (1) **Green Lantern** Photo © Photos 12/Alamy; p75 (2) **Green Lantern** courtesy of Warner Bros./DC Entertainment/The Kobal Collection; p75 (3) **Green Lantern** courtesy of Warner Bros./DC Entertainment/The Kobal Collection; p76 Courtesy of New Deal Pictures; p77 (2) Courtesy of Universal Studios Licensing LLC. ©2000 Universal City Studios Productions, Inc.; p77 (3) Photo by Dave J Hogan/WireImage; P78–79 "THE X-FILES" ©1998 Twentieth Century Fox. All rights reserved; p80 Photo © AF archive / Alamy; P81 **Batman Begins** courtesy of Warner Bros./D.C. Comics/The Kobal Collection/James, David; p82–83 Photo © AF archive/Alamy; p84–85 Photo © AF archive/Alamy; p86 Photo © Mike Kepka/San Francisco Chronicle/Corbis; p87 **Pirates of the Caribbean: Dead Man's Chest** courtesy of Walt Disney/The Kobal Collection; p88 Photo by Murray Close/Getty Images; p89 (2) Photo © AF archive/Alamy; p89 (3) Photo by Murray Close/Getty Images; p90 **Star Wars: Episode I—The Phantom Menace** courtesy of LucasFilm/The Kobal Collection; p91 **Star Wars: Episode I—The Phantom Menace** courtesy of LucasFilm/The Kobal Collection; p92 (1) **Pirates of the Caribbean: Curse of the Black Pearl** courtesy of Walt Disney/The Kobal Collection; p92 (2) **Pirates of the Caribbean: Curse of the Black Pearl** courtesy of Walt Disney/The Kobal Collection; p93 **Pirates of the Caribbean: Curse of the Black Pearl** courtesy of Walt Disney/The Kobal Collection; p94–95 **Pirates of the Caribbean: Dead Man's Chest** courtesy of Walt Disney/The Kobal Collection; p96 **Pacific Rim** courtesy of Legendary Pictures/The Kobal Collection; p97 **Pacific Rim** courtesy of Legendary Pictures/The Kobal Collection; p98 Photo by Christopher Polk/VF12/Getty Images for Vanity Fair; p99 **Titanic** courtesy of 20th Century Fox/Paramount/Digital Domain/The Kobal Collection; p101 (1) © Photos 12/Alamy; p101 (2) © Photos 12/Alamy; p102 **Titanic** courtesy of 20th Century Fox/Paramount/The Kobal Collection; p103 © AF archive/Alamy; p104 **The Aviator** courtesy of Warner Bros./The Kobal Collection; p105 **The Aviator** courtesy of Warner Bros./The Kobal Collection; p106 **Hugo** courtesy of GK Films/The Kobal Collection; p107 **Hugo** courtesy of GK Films/The Kobal Collection; p108 Courtesy of Weta Digital/Twentieth Century Fox; p109 **Rise of the Planet of the Apes** courtesy of Twentieth Century Fox Film/The Kobal Collection; p110 **The Lord of the Rings: The Return of the King** courtesy of New Line Cinema/The Kobal Collection; p111 **The Lord of the Rings: The Return of the King** courtesy of New Line Cinema/The Kobal Collection; p112 **The Hobbit: An Unexpected Journey** courtesy of New Line Cinema/The Kobal Collection; p113 **The Hobbit: An Unexpected Journey** courtesy of New Line Cinema/The Kobal Collection; p114 **King Kong** courtesy of Universal/Wing Nut Films/The Kobal Collection; p115 (2) **King Kong** courtesy of Universal/Wing Nut Films/The Kobal Collection; p115 (3) **King Kong** courtesy of Universal/Wing Nut Films/The Kobal Collection; p116 **Avatar** courtesy of Twentieth Century-Fox Film Corporation/The Kobal Collection; p117 **Avatar** courtesy of Twentieth Century-Fox Film Corporation/The Kobal Collection; p118 **Dawn of the Planet of the Apes** courtesy of Chernin Entertainment/The Kobal Collection; p119 (2) **Dawn of the Planet of the Apes** courtesy of Chernin Entertainment/The Kobal Collection; p119 (3) © Photos 12/Alamy; p120 Photo by Max Morse/WireImage; p121 **Young Sherlock Holmes** courtesy of Paramount/The Kobal Collection; p122–123 **Star Wars: Episode VI—Return of the Jedi** courtesy of LucasFilm/20th Century Fox/The Kobal Collection; p124 **Terminator 2: Judgment Day** courtesy of Carolco/The Kobal Collection; p125 © AF archive/Alamy; p126 © AF archive/Alamy; p127 **The Lost World** courtesy of Universal/Amblin/The Kobal Collection; p128 (1) **A.I. Artificial Intelligence** courtesy of

Amblin/Dreamworks/WB/The Kobal Collection; p128 (2) **A.I. Artificial Intelligence** courtesy of Amblin/Dreamworks/WB/The Kobal Collection; p129 **A.I. Artificial Intelligence** courtesy of Amblin/Dreamworks/WB/The Kobal Collection; p130 **War of the Worlds** courtesy of Dreamworks/Paramount/The Kobal Collection; p131 (2) **War of the Worlds** courtesy of Dreamworks/Paramount/The Kobal Collection; p131 (3) **War of the Worlds** courtesy of Dreamworks/Paramount/The Kobal Collection; p132 Lightstorm Entertainment. Courtesy of John Rosengrant; p133 **Terminator 2: Judgment Day** courtesy of Carolco/The Kobal Collection; p134 **Terminator 2: Judgment Day** courtesy of Carolco/The Kobal Collection; p135 **The Terminator** courtesy of Orion/The Kobal Collection; p136 © Louie Psihoyos/Corbis; p137 **Jurassic Park** courtesy of Amblin/Universal/The Kobal Collection; p138 (1) **Iron Man** courtesy of Marvel/Paramount/The Kobal Collection; p138 (2) **Iron Man 2** courtesy of Marvel/Paramount/The Kobal Collection; p139 **Iron Man** courtesy of Marvel/Paramount/The Kobal Collection; p140 **Real Steel** courtesy of Touchstone Pictures/The Kobal Collection; p141 (2) **Real Steel** courtesy of Touchstone Pictures/The Kobal Collection; p141 (3) **Real Steel** courtesy of Touchstone Pictures/The Kobal Collection; p142 Courtesy of Tippett Studio; p143 (2) **Star Wars: Episode V—The Empire Strikes Back** courtesy of LucasFilm/20th Century Fox/The Kobal Collection; p143 (3) **Star Wars: Episode VI—Return of the Jedi** courtesy of LucasFilm/20th Century Fox/The Kobal Collection; p144 **Star Wars: Episode VI—Return of the Jedi** courtesy of LucasFilm/20th Century Fox/The Kobal Collection; p145 © Douglas Kirkland/Corbis; p146 **Robocop** courtesy of Orion/The Kobal Collection; p147 **Robocop 2** courtesy of Orion/The Kobal Collection; p148 **Jurassic Park** courtesy of Amblin/Universal/The Kobal Collection; p149 **Jurassic Park** courtesy of Amblin/Universal/The Kobal Collection; p150 **Starship Troopers** courtesy of Columbia Tristar/The Kobal Collection; p151 **Starship Troopers** courtesy of Columbia Tristar/The Kobal Collection; p152–153 (1), (2), (3) **The Twilight Saga: Breaking Dawn—Part 1** and **The Twilight Saga: New Moon** courtesy of Summit Entertainment, LLC; p154 Courtesy of Trumbull Studios; p155 **Blade Runner** courtesy of Ladd Company/Warner Bros/The Kobal Collection; p156 **2001: A Space Odyssey** courtesy of MGM/The Kobal Collection; p157 (2) **2001: A Space Odyssey** courtesy of MGM/The Kobal Collection; p157 (3) Courtesy of Trumbull Studios; p158 **Close Encounters of the Third Kind** courtesy of Columbia/The Kobal Collection; p159 (2) **Close Encounters of the Third Kind** courtesy of Columbia/The

Kobal Collection; p159 (3) **Close Encounters of the Third Kind** courtesy of Columbia/The Kobal Collection; p160 **Star Trek** courtesy of Paramount/The Kobal Collection; p161 (2) **Star Trek** courtesy of Paramount/The Kobal Collection; p161 (3) **Star Trek** courtesy of Paramount/The Kobal Collection; p162 **Blade Runner** courtesy of Ladd Company/Warner Bros/The Kobal Collection; p163 **Blade Runner** courtesy of Ladd Company/Warner Bros/The Kobal Collection; p164 Photo by Valerie Macon/Getty Images; p165 **Life of Pi** courtesy of Fox 2000 Pictures/Dune Entertainment/Ingenious Media/Haishang Films/The Kobal Collection; p166 **Babe: Pig in the City** courtesy of Universal City Studios/The Kobal Collection/Mill Film; p167 **Babe: Pig in the City** courtesy of Universal City Studios/The Kobal Collection/Johns, Carolyn; p168 **Chronicles of Narnia: The Lion, the Witch, and the Wardrobe** courtesy of Walt Disney Pictures/Walden Media/The Kobal Collection/Bray, Phil; p169 **Chronicles of Narnia: The Lion, the Witch, and the Wardrobe** courtesy of Walt Disney Pictures/Walden Media/The Kobal Collection; p170 **The Golden Compass** courtesy of New Line Cinema/The Kobal Collection; p171 **The Golden Compass** courtesy of New Line Cinema/The Kobal Collection; p172 **Life of Pi** courtesy of Fox 2000 Pictures/Dune Entertainment/Ingenious Media/Haishang Films/The Kobal Collection; p173 (2) **Life of Pi** courtesy of Fox 2000 Pictures/Dune Entertainment/Ingenious Media/Haishang Films/The Kobal Collection; p173 (3) © Photos 12/Alamy; p174 Photo by Valerie Macon/Getty Images; p175 (2) **Captain America: The First Avenger** courtesy of Marvel/Paramount/The Kobal Collection; p175 (3) **Captain America: The First Avenger** courtesy Marvel/Paramount/The Kobal Collection; p176 © Photos 12/Alamy; p177 "X-MEN: THE LAST STAND" © 2006 Twentieth Century Fox. All Rights Reserved; p178 **The Curious Case of Benjamin Button** courtesy of Paramount Pictures/Warner Bros. Pictures/The Kobal Collection; p179 **The Curious Case of Benjamin Button** courtesy of Paramount Pictures/Warner Bros. Pictures/The Kobal Collection; p180 © AF archive/Alamy; p181 Courtesy of Edson Williams; p182–183 © 2014 Marvel Studios. Marvel's **Captain America: The Winter Soldier** Images appear Courtesy of Marvel Studios; p191 **Jurassic Park** courtesy of Amblin/Universal/The Kobal Collection.

Acknowledgments

These 16 special and visual effects supervisors who participated in recounting stories of their careers generously made time for interviews and correspondence from across the world: John Bruno, Chris Corbould, Richard Edlund, Scott Farrar, Paul Franklin, Karen Goulekas, Ian Hunter, John Knoll, Robert Legato, Joe Letteri, Dennis Muren, John Rosengrant, Phil Tippett, Douglas Trumbull, Bill Westenhofer, and Edson Williams.

Several people from effects studios helped to co-ordinate interviews and gather imagery: Diana Godo, Dave Gouge, Greg Grusby, Sarah Harries, Stephen Kenneally, Emily Kwong, Lori Petrini, Niketa Roman, Corey Rosen, Cole Taylor, and Leslie Valladares.

The Ilex team at OPG provided incredible guidance and were always a helpful voice on the end of the phone: Zara Larcombe, Commissioning Editor, and in particular my Editor, Natalia Price-Cabrera.

A huge thank you also to director James Cameron and producer Lorenzo di Bonaventura for generously writing such fantastic forewords in record time. Thank you to Sharon Swart for reaching out to Lorenzo and helping to facilitate things. Thank you too to director Duncan Jones for endorsing this book.

Thanks must go to Lauretta Dives and Darren Thomas at Picture Desk for their patience and open-ended help regarding image requests for this book.

I would not have had the chance to write this book or have had access to the effects supervisors of such high stature without being given a start in visual effects journalism by Mike Seymour, John Montgomery, and Jeff Heusser at fxguide.

Family and friends were instrumental in offering advice and encouragement and putting up with my endless discussion about special and visual effects: Sue Bennett, Geoff Failes, Penny Failes, Joanna Failes, Paul Erickson, Savvas Pertsinidis, James Shen, and Danyl Traynor.

Thousands of effects artists contribute to films, television shows, commercials, computer games, and other forms of entertainment—I am inspired by their work every day.